next

next

next

LIVING FOR JESUS IN
THE REAL WORLD

MATT CARVEL

10 Publishing
a division of 10ofthose.com

First published in Great Britain in 2017

British Library Cataloguing in Publication Data
A record for this book is available from the British Library

ISBN: 978-1-911272-61-8

Designed by Mike Thorpe / www.design-chapel.com

Printed in Denmark by Nørhaven

10Publishing, a division of 10ofthose.com
Unit C, Tomlinson Road, Leyland, PR25 2DY, England
Email: info@10ofthose.com
Website: www.10ofthose.com

Contents

Introduction:

Even Superman Can't Do It

I believe in Christianity as I believe that the sun has risen: not only because I see it, but because by it I see everything else.
C.S. Lewis

This great quotation is familiar to many but is particularly memorable for me because it connects belief in Christianity to the realities of day-to-day life. Does that connection seem like an obvious one to you? If we believe that Jesus is God's Son, that He died for our sins and that He rose to give us eternal life (1 Cor. 15:3–4), of course that will change how we live! But, in my experience, the extent to which this 'life-changing' truth cannot change someone's life is also remarkable.

I'm not talking just about 'someone else' here – I've experienced it personally too. I've been a Christian since I was a child but that doesn't mean my beliefs have informed the way I have lived for all that time. In fact there's been significant parts of my life where I've intentionally tried to keep 'what I believe' and 'the way I live' very separate. You can just about manage it too, for a while at least. But in the end living a 'double life' is too much for one person to sustain – even Superman struggles with it! Many of us have had to learn this the hard way.

In my late teens I had decided that I wanted to live my own life and make decisions with me, rather than God, at the centre. What became most important in my life was being cool, girls, playing rock and roll, and drinking with my friends. If I'm honest, I wanted to be a rock star (part of me still does) and live the rock star life. I thought I was doing quite well at first too. I formed a band, I was lead singer and my popularity in school shot up a fair bit. I got a girlfriend and spent a great deal of time at parties and clubs, having fun and drinking quite a lot. But although on the surface things were going quite well, inside I was tearing myself apart. I was still attending church on a Sunday and in the back of my mind I knew Christianity was true. Though a strong part of me wanted to turn my back on it, I never fully could. Outwardly I was living the party lifestyle but internally a real conflict was raging.

I remember waking up one morning after a particularly heavy night and feeling too ill to move. My mum came in, as I was still living at home at the time, and she was clearly upset about the way I was behaving. She could tell that things weren't going well for me either, despite the impression that I wanted to give to my friends. As I lay motionless on my bed, I vividly remember her saying to me, 'He wants you all.' I knew she was right. God wasn't satisfied with part of my life. This was the real source of tension inside of me. Deep down I knew that I was made for God (Col. 1:16). I knew that what Jesus had done for me on the cross was more important than any girlfriend, popularity or wild night that I could gain for myself. God loved me to such an extent that He wanted me to give Him every part of my life (Rom. 12:1) – not just my Sunday mornings. In time God completely turned my life around. It was – and still is – a process, but that moment was a significant step on the journey.

The reality is that the temptation to believe one

thing and do another is always with us. We live in a broken world that is filled with people who don't prioritise Jesus Christ because really they don't know anything about Him. Therefore fitting in with everyone else and living like they do is the easy road that often looks very appealing. Maybe, like me, you've been tempted to keep your 'spiritual life' and 'everyday life' separate. However, as C.S. Lewis says in that quotation, the Gospel is not meant to be a single aspect of our lives; it's supposed to be the light that helps us see everything.

That is what this book is all about: letting the light of God's Word shine onto every aspect of our lives. As I have said, I have not always made the right decisions in my life and learnt many lessons the hard way. Maybe you won't agree with every conclusion I come to about what the Bible says and how we should apply that in specific situations. But if this book helps you to connect your day-to-day life with God's truth, then it has achieved its purpose.

Part One:
How to Do Life Well

1

Freedom

Whoever finds their life will lose it, and whoever loses their life for my sake will find it.
Matthew 10:39

In my first book, *First*, I attempted to answer the question: 'How do you live for Jesus at university?' Its intended audience, therefore, was Christian students. I have written this next book (creatively named, I know) with two types of people in mind. First, Christian students who are about to finish university or have recently graduated and are facing the question: 'How do you live for Jesus in the *real world*?' As I began writing, I realised that there are also many other people who ask the same question, not because they have recently graduated – they have already been living in 'the real world', probably for some time – but because they have recently become Christians. How to view work, decisions and the complexities of the real world (as opposed to the unique and slightly sheltered experience of university) in light of the Gospel is a question that a wide audience should, and indeed do, ask. Therefore this book is aimed secondly at new Christian believers.

So whether you're starting out on a post-university life or a new life with Jesus, my aim is to help you connect the eternal truth of what the Bible says with the challenges, opportunities and decisions that you will face. Incidentally, you may like to read my previous book even if you're not or have never been a student, as I've deliberately not overlapped any content with this one. Several of the topics in it are not university specific. (Shameless plug over …) My message in this book, as it was in *First*, is that putting Jesus first in every area of our lives is far and away the best thing to do. It is never easy and there are great costs involved but it is the path of life (Matt. 7:14).

If you're reading this book, I'm assuming that you're interested in living such a life, so let me give you some words of warning right at the beginning. It's likely that the majority of people you'll meet in life view living for Jesus as a very stupid thing to do. They may not say that to your face, but they may well think that living according to principles written thousands of years ago is a sign that you've probably lost your mind.

Living by God's Word can produce such a strong reaction in people because most, especially in a country like ours, prize personal freedom as the greatest of all values. Any suggestion that someone would give up this freedom in order to obey and submit to someone else, especially God, is considered at best idiotic and at worst a dangerous threat to national security.

When I talk about personal freedom, I'm talking about the attitude of 'it's my life; I can do what I like'. In other words, it's the attitude that you are not accountable to anyone – let alone a Creator God – for the decisions you make. You will no doubt have encountered this a lot. In fact, it is so ingrained in our society, many people don't even realise that it's the idea that drives all their decisions! Through social media, advertising, films, music and in so many other ways we're constantly presented with the powerful idea that *if we exercise our personal freedom in exactly the way we want, we will be happy*. Thus we are encouraged to find our satisfaction in this world. We are to be independent; express our individuality; not let other people suppress us; buy what we want to buy; live where we want to live; pursue what we want to pursue. In short if it feels right, go for it! And if we do this, we'll be happy. And everyone wants to be happy, right?

The problem is this kind of freedom doesn't bring happiness in a lasting way at all. The Bible is clear that humankind's purpose – and where we find fulfilment – is to love God wholeheartedly and glorify Him by the way we live (Ecc. 12:13; Matt. 22:37–38). Why should we think creation will satisfy our desire for happiness rather than the Creator – especially as our Creator invites us into an eternal relationship with Himself through Jesus Christ? The world sees the pursuit of personal freedom as wise and good, but God condemns it as foolishness (Rom. 1:18–32).

At certain points in my life, this worldly pursuit is one I have wholeheartedly made my own. In doing so I have personally experienced the futility and emptiness of the world's claims to 'wisdom'. As I explained in the introduction, for years I pursued my own idea of freedom but it didn't lead to happiness as I thought it would. I tried to be popular and successful, and lived life regardless of the consequences. On the surface it looked like I had done pretty well. But when I became popular, I also became anxious that I'd lose my approval. When I had some measure of success, the next rung on the ladder became far more important than what I had achieved. Pursuing 'fun' and living without the consequences was great for a while at least, but I still felt empty and shallow – it didn't justify my existence (which was what I was really looking for). I wanted to be free and happy, and I ended up enslaved to the pursuit of freedom and miserable.

Now, I'm not saying that everyone who doesn't follow Jesus will end up being miserable. Life isn't as black and white as that. Rather, I'm saying that the 'pursuit of personal freedom' that is so widely embraced by people in Western cultures is not bringing people the happiness they expect. The United States is the country that prides itself on being the 'land of the free' but it also has the highest rate of depression in the world.*

So while giving up aspects of our personal freedom to follow Christ will maybe sound extreme, restrictive and unpleasant to people, the alternative is that, without God, we just have to make life up as we go along. And who made us the experts on life anyway? This is one reason why many people are so confused about what they should do in life and how they should live – because they refuse to ask their Creator what life is all about. Imagine if your car decided it wanted to be a boat. Imagine if your TV decided to be a bread maker. Imagine if your shoes decided to be gloves … I think you get the point: things are made for a purpose! It's no wonder that when human beings decide to ignore their Maker and find their own meaning to and purpose for life themselves, it doesn't work out as well as they hoped.

The reality is that inventing meaning is what people do every day. If you ask your friends who aren't Christians about their lives, you'll notice that they use trial and error to find a way to make their

* *Taken from the World Health Organisation's report 'Age-standardized DALYs per 100,000 by cause, and member state' (2004).*

lives work. Regardless of what moral rules they may choose, they're essentially making up their guiding principles as they go along. They don't really have a clear idea about what life is about. They may have some ideas that life should be about being good, helping people and making the world a better place; maybe they just want to be happy and make the best of it. But when I've asked why they think that, I've not heard one answer that really satisfies the question.

If we're going to put Jesus first, we're going to have to reject this prevalent and powerful idea that 'personal freedom brings happiness'. It may be convenient; it may appeal to our instincts and urges. But it is an enslaving and sinful lie (John 8:34) that promises much and delivers little.

We may not realise it at first but what we give our life to ends up enslaving us. Make popularity your aim and you'll always crave a little more respect and appreciation. Make success your aim and there will always be someone better than you, richer than you and who has achieved more than you. Even if you make contentment and peace your aim, the things that are out of your control will strip it away from you. Just the fear of losing what you've gained in life is enough to ruin everything.

If I'm going to be enslaved to something, I'd gladly choose that to be Christ (Rom. 6:20–23). By this I mean that I willingly accept Jesus as the boss of my life. Living this way is not always an easy road

– it will often involve sacrificing my own desires. But I know that He alone brings true freedom – not the freedom to do what I want, but freedom from sin, guilt and anxiety, and the freedom that comes from knowing peace with God. This is what Jesus is describing in Matthew 10:39: when we lose our lives for Christ's sake, we find the freedom that comes from knowing our true purpose in life. There's real freedom in knowing where we came from and where we're going to; being content in God is the deepest and most joyful contentment that exists (Ps. 16:11).

Living for Christ in the real world does feel like a great sacrifice at times. It can feel like a frontal assault on our 'personal freedom', and in fact that's exactly what it is. But if we really know God, we know that the path of 'personal freedom' – the path that so many people around us may be running down with huge smiles on their faces – doesn't lead to a good place anyway. What's more, Jesus makes an incredible promise to us: not only is He with us each step of the way on our road, but anything that we do lose, give up or have to endure for His sake will not be unrewarded in the end (Matt. 19:29). Life makes us many offers but there really is no better one than that.

2

Love

This book is mainly about making important decisions and living for God in every aspect of our lives. Before I get into the practicalities of that, though, let's pause and reflect on the significance of our lives because God's love for us is the truth that shapes our lives and all the decisions that we make.

One of the enemy's most effective tricks is to try to convince us that our lives are unimportant. In the very beginning he tempted Adam and Eve to think that the consequences of their actions wouldn't be as significant as God had said they would be (Gen. 3:1–5). He has continued in this pattern ever since and is called 'the father of lies' (John 8:44).

Likewise we can undervalue our own significance, though this might sound like humility: 'I'm just a simple Christian who struggles through life.' Of course, we all struggle with sin (1 John 1:8) and we should be sober-minded in our assessment of ourselves (Rom. 12:3). But if we're not careful, we can fall into the enemy's trap and believe his lies: 'Does it *really* matter if you sin? Does anyone really care? You're a struggling sinner – sinning is just what you do.' Have you ever had thoughts like that? Similarly have you ever questioned God's call on your life: how can I do anything significant for God? He probably doesn't expect very much of me – I'm not a 'great Christian' – or isn't going to use me very much.

Our lives and the decisions we make – from the everyday, mundane ones as we battle with sin and choose God's way, to the big, life-shaping ones – are all incredibly significant to God. God loved us from before He created the world and has specifically chosen us to be part of His family (Eph. 1:4–5). We are all children of God (Rom. 8:16) and so should never think that we are insignificant to God or that He prefers certain children more than others. We have been not only forgiven of our sin but saved by God's grace for a life of purposeful service to Him (Eph. 2:10). These are just a few examples but the New Testament is full of similar statements about our identity in Christ. God wants us to be totally confident in who we are in Him (2 Cor. 5:17) and these truths are a protection against the lies of Satan (Eph. 6:11).

God's love for us is such a simple truth, albeit an infinitely powerful one, that we can easily take it for granted. That's why the Bible reminds us to keep ourselves in the love of God (Jude 21). It's not that our behaviour or our circumstances can cause us to lose His love (Rom. 8:35–39) but that we can lose our enjoyment and appreciation of God's love if our life become overly fixated on the concerns of the day.

Are you confident in God's love for you? How would you feel about going up to a Christian friend right now and saying, 'God really loves me!'? Would that feel strange? Would you feel embarrassed about it? Do you truly believe it? If you are a Christian, Jesus Christ has loved you so much that He has given His life for you (Gal. 2:20). If you are going to put Him first in your life, you need to embrace, enjoy and revel in this truth constantly.

I labour this point because many Christians think that living the Christian life is about our love for God – they assume that as sinners, saved only by God's grace, we shouldn't focus on ourselves but on God and serving Him. I completely agree that our life should be God-orientated not self-orientated, but at the same time we must be careful that 'living for God's glory' doesn't become 'trying hard to behave well for Him'. If we end up there, we've missed the point. You see, it's possible to be so focused on serving and obeying God that enjoying God's love for us becomes neglected in our Christian experience. We must remember that God's love comes first (1 John 4:19). We love because He first loved us, and by extension the more God's love fills our hearts and minds, the more love we have to give back to God and to others. Jesus said that only if we abide in Him will we be fruitful for Him (John 15:5).

This book does not contain much advice or instruction about reading the Bible and praying each day because I gave a good amount of time to them in *First*. However, I do want to underline how important they are in the Christian life. As well as enabling us to get to know God better and deepen our relationship by talking and listening to Him, these are essential opportunities for us to enjoy and bask in God's love for us. I know in my life that the days I neglect to remind myself of God's love and the goodness of the Gospel I am much more vulnerable to sin and temptation, failing to demonstrate God's love to others in my thoughts, words and actions. When I do take the time to be with God, I realise that my life, and the choices I make today, are incredibly significant. Each one of my sins nailed Jesus to the cross (Is. 53:5) and yet He gladly went there to die for me and forgive me (Heb. 12:2). As a loved child of God I can offer my life back to Him not out of a sense of obligation but out of worship to Him (Rom. 12:1).

To love God is the first and greatest commandment (Matt. 22:37–38) but unless we prioritise being loved by God, we won't do 'loving God' very well. When we realise and regularly remind ourselves that out of all the people who have ever lived God chose us, individually, to be with Him (Eph. 1:5) and spend eternity with Him (John 14:2), we begin to understand just how significant our lives are. Only then can we effectively live lives of purpose for His glory.

God doesn't love us because we make the right decisions or serve Him well or find the 'right career' or witness for Him zealously. He loves us first. The significance of our lives comes from that fact and nothing else. All around us there are people wondering if their life is truly significant. Some are trying to feel significant by pursuing relationships with others. Some are trying to make themselves significant by forging brilliant careers or earning lots of money. The Christian gets his or her significance from what God has already done for them – we are eternally significant to Him. Anything we do in life does not add to or change that one bit.

Everything I encourage you to do through this book should come as a heart response to God's love for you. We're not trying to be 'super Christians' or 'win at life'; we're simply trying to navigate our lives in a way that honours Him because we're so bowled over with His incredible love for us.

3

Success

So far I have said that putting Jesus first in life is about allowing the light of His Word to shine on every aspect of what we do. It's very different, and ultimately much more rewarding, than pursuing personal freedom like many others do. It's a life that is motivated by God's amazing love for us. But how do we do it? How can we be successful at living for God in the real world? If you have ever tried to do so, you'll know it's not easy, but the good news is that there are steps you can take that will really help. The first stage of succeeding in living for God is to begin working at it!

Let me explain using this illustration. I've heard it said that one of the reasons people enjoy great performances is that in our minds we pretend that we are taking part. As we watch a great singer or dancer or actor, we're fantasising about us performing in the same way. We're enjoying the idea of being so talented and of receiving the praise and adulation that comes with it. I'm sure it's something we all do from time to time, whether we like to admit it or not.

But experiences like this can work both ways. We might enjoy imagining such a scenario but we can also become discouraged that it never will happen in reality! The other day I was listening to the radio and a song came on that I had never heard before. Immediately the words and music grabbed me and I thought, 'That's a great song.' In my time I've written a few songs and dabbled in music to some extent. Therefore for me hearing a great song can create the rather confusing effect of both inspiring me and at the same time causing me to despairingly think, 'I wish I had written that song!'

When it comes to the Christian life, we can be inspired and discouraged in a similar way. We encounter someone that we regard as a great Christian – often a church leader, a longstanding member of our church or someone we read about – and we want to be like them. Maybe we want to speak about the Gospel the way they do or pray with the boldness and passion that they have. Maybe we see their kindness and hospitality or patience and grace and think, 'I wish I could be like that!'

Every true Christian has a desire to become

more like Jesus, even if this is hidden amongst lots of other competing desires in our hearts. But this can lead us to discouragement when we find it hard to see how we'll ever be as mature, loving, gracious, patient and prayerful as other Christians. This is especially the case when we're trying to imitate their behaviour rather than learn from the journey that took them to where they are today.

The journey is often more important than we realise. With that song I heard on the radio, it just so happened that once it had finished the artist was there in the studio with the radio DJ and began discussing his career. 'Well, I arrived in Nashville two years ago,' he said. (It's country music I was listening to by the way – don't judge me!) 'And I was trying to make it as a songwriter. So for two years I wrote song after song after song, listened to the best artists I could find and tried to learn how to do it.' The song he had just played was a very simple one. You might hear it and think it took him only ten minutes to write – and maybe it did. But in reality it had taken him two years of full-time songwriting.

His story could have been very different. He could have tried writing songs for a while, found that he couldn't create anything very good and concluded, 'Well, I guess songwriting is just not for me.' But he didn't. He had a dream and he pursued it relentlessly. He quit his job, moved house and lived like a pauper just so he could give his whole life to writing songs. Two years later his songs are starting to make it onto the radio.

G.K. Chesterton once famously wrote, 'The Christian ideal has not been tried and found wanting. It has been found difficult; and left untried.' We all want to be godlier Christians, but often trying to change in this way feels like a lot of effort and it's hard to see progress being made. After a week or a month or even a year we still struggle the way we used to. We go to church, we try to read our Bibles and pray but it seems to make little difference. We might be tempted to give up or at least give up hope that we'll ever really change. We might make all sorts of excuses to justify this too: 'I'm just like that ... This sin is my Achilles' heel ... I'll never be as prayerful/generous/evangelistic as them because that's not my gifting ... If you knew my background, you'd know it's impossible for me to change in this area.'

Those excuses are exactly that: excuses. They're all pathetic and, more importantly, they contradict God's Word. God says that we will change 'from one degree of glory to another' (2 Cor. 3:18, ESV); this, then, is what can and will happen in our lives. If Paul can say, 'I can do all this through him [Christ] who gives me strength' (Phil. 4:13), then we can too. God's will for our lives is sanctification (1 Thes. 4:3) – that's the journey mapped out for us. God has started a good work in us and we can be completely confident that He will bring it to completion (Phil. 1:6).

Many people dream of being great musicians but take no steps to actually realising that goal. Most people imagine that successful people are those who have been touched with a magic wand called 'talent'; for the rest of us there's no point in trying. But speak to successful people about their life and you'll find out how untrue that is. Although they do have some 'natural' abilities that get them started, the effort that they put in, the sacrifices that they make and the hours of practice that they endure are the real reason for their success.

In the Christian life there are no 'talented' people when it comes to the journey of sanctification. We're all equally lost in our sin without Jesus, we have all been born again because of Him and we all have been made by God for good works (Eph. 2:1–9). If you analyse the life of any Christian you admire or any Christian in history who has achieved great things for God, you'll see that their 'success' was the tip of the iceberg. Their practice day after day of relating to God and being shaped more and more by Him and His Word – through obedience, prayer and worship – is largely unseen but is the secret to their 'success'. Moreover, often it cost them a great deal and they had to make many sacrifices in order to reach their goal of knowing God better.

There are many different definitions of what a successful life looks like, but for a Christian this journey of sanctification brings about the greatest success of all: spiritual fruitfulness. The good news is that this is God's calling for us and He has promised to do what is necessary to lead us on the journey. The not-so-good news is that it is a journey, not a simple technique we can master in an afternoon. It is a journey that takes time, effort, sacrifice and faith. No tree can produce fruit overnight and the fruit of the Spirit (Gal. 5:22–23) doesn't grow at that speed either. To become spiritually fruitful, we must become deeply rooted in God (John 15:5) and this involves developing a relationship with Him over a lifetime.

In the next section we'll begin looking at the practicalities of making big decisions that will shape the course of our lives. But it's important to remember that while where we live and work and who we choose to share our lives with are big decisions, they are not the ultimate decisions. These things provide the context and setting for life's central pursuit of becoming more like Jesus. This is God's will for our lives. So many people, sadly even some Christians, act as if having a great career or being wealthy, married or admired is what life is all about. Yet God reminds us that none of these things will last; only our relationship with God lasts forever. The rewards we gain from prioritising that now, even though it can be challenging, are infinitely worthwhile.

Part Two:
How to Make Good Decisions

4

What is God's Will for My Life?

'How many hours, days, weeks, even years have Christians agonised over that question? It might well be a very pressing question for you right now if you have just finished university or have recently become a Christian. It is also a really good question to ask because it acknowledges that obeying God is the best thing to do in life, that God does have plans for you and that He cares enough to want to communicate them to you.

It is worth dwelling on this for a moment. There are seven billion people in the world but God cares about each one of us. If we each turned to Him and listened, God would be able to lead us all on an amazing journey that is tailor-made for our good (Rom. 8:28). What a God!

However, though all of us should ask this question, working out the answer is often not straightforward. Looking to God's Word is obviously a great place to start, but we quickly realise that although the Bible is God's primary way of speaking to us, He's not addressed each of us by name in it. As much as we might want it, there's no appendix to the Bible that lists the name of every Christian and then describes what God wants them to do, where they should live, what church they should attend, and so on.

However, sometimes we act as if such an appendix does exist. Many Christians live with the idea that a list with the details of our life is sitting on God's desk up in heaven and that He is waiting for us to act it out. Some even live with the fear of God's disapproval if they make a decision that contradicts this specific plan.

Perhaps you have never thought or acted like that, but I can understand from where the idea might come. It seems reasonable to suppose that 'God's will' is quite detailed about the important aspects of our life. When we read books like Isaiah, the expanse of God's wisdom and knowledge is overwhelming:

I am God, and there is no other;
I am God, and there is none like me.
I make known the end from the beginning,
from ancient times, what is still to come.
Isaiah 46:9–10

History is entirely held in God's hands; He knows it inside out. From landmark moments in political history to natural disasters to the feelings and emotions that we experience day by day, He knows it all. Everything that has happened, is happening and will happen is simultaneously intimately seen by our amazing God.

When we consider God's knowledge and try to apply this truth to our lives, it is tempting to follow a thought process like this. First, God knows everything, including the future. Second, God cares about us and what we do in life. Third, we therefore conclude, God has a very specific list of things that we're supposed to do and be; we're supposed to discern exactly what they are and then do them entirely. Yet such thinking can make us so worried about missing a path that we're 'supposed' to go down that we lose any sense of trust in our loving, wise Father to direct our steps. The fact that God has a will for our lives can become a difficult burden rather than a comforting truth!

But although the Bible does affirm the first and second points in many places, we must realise that the third point is a logical conclusion we come to rather than something that God specifically says. It's true that there are many examples of God speaking explicitly to someone about their life in the Bible. God speaks to Abraham about going to a new land and his family becoming a great nation (Gen. 12); God speaks to Moses through the burning bush and tells him to lead the Israelites out of Egypt (Ex. 3); and God speaks to Saul, later called Paul, in a way that totally turns his life upside down, changing him from a persecutor of the church to its most fruitful missionary (Acts 9). But is this normal?

Reading stories like these can cause us to wait for our own 'Damascus road' or 'burning bush' moment. The idea can slip into our heads that this is the only or main way that God reveals His will and He's about to speak to us in a similar way. But these incidents are in the Bible because they are exceptional moments in the history of God's salvation plan for the world. Yes, God had some specific directions to give these people at these times, but that doesn't mean this is the normal way God operates with everyone.

If we read these stories carefully, we'll see that these moments were even exceptional in the lives of the men themselves. God wasn't constantly telling them what to do. Take Abraham, for example. He had a real sense of God's purpose over his life. He was going to be the father of a great nation and carry the blessing of God for generations to come. But even these promises and direction are still quite broad. God gave no timeframe; there were no specifics about how it was going to happen. So there was plenty of room for Abraham to do silly things and make mistakes. He conceives a son called Ishmael with a woman who isn't his wife, and he pretends that his wife is actually his sister, which means she nearly gets married to another man!

In fact it seems Abraham does a fairly good job of getting in the way of 'God's plan'. But the point is that God's plan does come to fruition. In the end God achieves what He wants to achieve. In the meantime, though, God gives Abraham – just as He does with Moses, Paul, me and you – plenty of room to make his own decisions and even get it wrong sometimes. You see, God does care about us and He does know our futures, but 'His will' is big and wide, leaving us plenty of room to make our own decisions.

As I have already explained, the main objective of God's will for our lives is our sanctification. We may not have a 'burning bush' moment in our lives, but that doesn't mean God hasn't spoken to us about our lives and destiny. He has made this clear in black and white. So as we try to discern any other way God might be leading or guiding us in the decisions that we make, it is important to have this understanding in mind.

Knowing this gives us the freedom to make decisions and hopefully saves us from unnecessary worry about our futures. It is a great comfort. Yet it is still natural for us to pray and seek God for direction about big decisions that we must make. Is there a path we can take that will be more beneficial than others? How and where can we glorify God most and bear most spiritual fruit?

These are great questions to ask, and the truth is that one of those options may well be more beneficial than the others. But when we ask such questions, we sometimes have an unhelpful picture in mind of certain paths being right and other paths being wrong. For example, imagine the career options that are currently open to you are becoming an accountant, a maths teacher or a social worker. You could see yourself doing any of them, so how do you choose? Does God have a preference? Is one right and the others wrong? It's as if you've been following a path through a jungle and suddenly it splits three ways. But you can't see very far down any of the routes, so how do you know which one God want you to take? Although the Bible doesn't present the idea of 'God's will' being a career choice – and, as with Abraham, Moses and Paul, God gives us plenty of room to make our own decisions – how do we get closer to a decision if we're faced with a number of options?

Psalm 119:105 says, 'Your word is a lamp for my feet, a light on my path.' This is a great description of how God helps us through life. Notice that it doesn't say, 'Your word is a signpost' or 'a list of specific directions for travel'. No, God's Word is a 'lamp'; it helps to illuminate our situation in order that we can make good decisions.

So to return to our example, is being an accountant, a maths teacher or a social worker the best thing to do? The correct course of action is to ask God, to read His Word for guidance, to submit your heart to Him so that you are driven by loving Him and then to make a decision. Often God's leading doesn't seem that clear to us at the time. Sometimes it's only years later that we look back and can recognise what He was doing in us. But by being open to Him by reading His Word and praying, and by taking a step of faith even if we don't feel 100 per cent sure, we are honouring Him in the process.

While some jobs would be immoral or unwise for us to pursue, we have the freedom to choose between many others. Also there's something more glorifying to God about submitting our decisions to Him in this way than if God treated us like slaves that He orders about. God's priority is that we obey Him day by day, learn to depend on Him and become more like Him by deepening our relationship with Him. God can use the varied paths we choose to sanctify us (even if they're not always the wisest choices) and what's more He uses the process of making decisions to deepen our trust in Him too.

I've heard it put like this: 'God's will is a compass rather than a map.' I think this is helpful and in line with what the Bible says. Of course, sometimes God does speak to us very specifically when we're faced with a decision. We might one day have a strong sense that one direction is right. After thinking it through, praying about it and asking for advice, we might realise this really is God prompting us about a specific path. Yet while not wanting to undermine God working in this way from time to time, often we try to seek a specific answer from God when all He wants to do is point our lives in a general direction – growing in Christ-likeness – and allow us to take the necessary steps.

5

How Do I Obey God's Will?

Whatever stage we're at in life, we all face big decisions from time to time. Even if our life is quite settled in terms of our job, location and relationships, we sometimes wonder whether we're doing the right thing and what life would be like if we headed down a different path. If we're a Christian, this will hopefully lead us to ask, 'What is God's will for my life?'

As I said in the previous chapter, though, we need to be clear about our understanding of 'God's will'. It's often unhelpful to attach the label to specific choices we need to make, such as about a job or a house. The Bible uses the term 'God's will' quite differently, for example declaring, 'It is God's will that you should be sanctified' (1 Thes. 4:3).

To return to the thought process I mentioned at the end of the last chapter, we may be clear that God knows everything and also that He cares about us and what we do in life. Yet instead of concluding, 'God has a specific list of things He wants us to fulfil in life', this Bible verse shows us that a better understanding is that '*whatever* we do and *wherever* we are, and even if we make mistakes along the way, God is committed to making us more like Jesus'. That's amazing, isn't it? This is the goal that God is constantly working towards and it's much more significant than anything else in our lives.

When we're faced with big decisions, the weight of them can quickly overwhelm us if we're not careful. As we dwell on the benefits, costs and potential implications, we can be preoccupied for days or weeks at a time. Yes, we are to seek to align our decisions with God's will for us – that of becoming more like Jesus. We should think carefully about which path fits more with God's big plan of what He is doing with His people. But we must remember that just because something seems – on the surface – pressing and urgent to us, that doesn't mean that God feels the same way about it. He's concerned because He's our loving heavenly Father, yet this decision will almost certainly not 'make or break' our lives. What's most important to God is that we become more like Jesus.

We are urged in 1 Peter 5:7: 'Cast all your anxiety on him because he cares for you.' This does not mean just trying to forget about our worries for a while; it's about seeing life from God's perspective. The Bible reminds us He *cares* about us deeply. We don't need to fret and worry like other people who don't know God because we can trust that He will provide for us, guide us and even rescue us when things go wrong (Ps. 37:24). Of course God is interested in the decisions we have to make, but reminding ourselves that God is committed to His purpose for our lives no matter which path we take can hugely take the pressure off.

This is what sanctification is all about: becoming more like Jesus day by day. It's what God thinks is important *all the time*. You may not feel that God is giving you specific instructions about what to do right now but that's not because God doesn't care about you. God is 100 per cent committed to fulfilling His will in your life (Phil. 1:6). Though it might seem surprising, His will for your life is not really about what job you're going to do, who you might marry or whether you will be single your whole life. God's will is that you become like Him more and more – and He can use every situation or circumstance to accomplish that.

Later on in 1 Thessalonians Paul gives another definition of 'God's will' and this time adds specifics about what we should be doing: 'Rejoice always, pray continually, give thanks in all circumstances;

for this is God's will for you in Christ Jesus' – (1 Thes. 5:16–18).

When we're faced with a big decision, this is probably not the type of advice we're looking for, if we're honest. But again, although we can become obsessed with the practical short-term implications of our choices, God is mostly concerned with the deeper, long-term maturing of our inner selves. Rejoicing, praying and giving thanks cultivates joy, patience, dependence on God and even spiritual power in our lives. That is, in so many ways, a much better answer to our prayers than which option we should choose when we make a decision.

God's will is, in fact, no doubt a lot better than we. He's not a Magic 8-Ball – a toy for giving advice. He's a Father who cares about making us more like His Son. It's time to put down the idea that 'God's will' is a hoop we need to jump through, and realise that God works His will in our lives in *all circumstances*. That's pretty amazing. Stop and think about that for a minute.

No, really, stop reading and ponder that brilliant truth. Are you ready to respond to it yet?

We live in a world that gauges success by what we achieve: how far up the career ladder we get; how much money we earn; how big our house is; what car we drive; how talented people think we are. The list goes on. When we're making big decisions, it's tempting to think in this way too. We think about what other people will say. We worry that we'll 'fall behind' in life. We dwell far too long on what we might be able to afford with our potential salary. Alternatively we're flattered a little too much by the new respect a certain title might give us. Yet God measures success not by what we *gain* in life but by the manner in which we live it out.

God's will isn't taking a specific path; it's that we say, 'I will' to Him each day. This is how we become like Jesus: by obeying Him, which brings us closer to Him. God's promise to us is that if we put following Him first, He'll take care of everything else (Matt. 6:31–34).

Are you so concerned about 'God's will for your future' that you've forgotten about God's will for you today? Living with God's perspective helps us see our workplace, our friendships and our day-to-day lives in a totally different light. We start asking ourselves questions such as: 'Who can I show God's love to?' 'Who can I serve?' 'Who should I pray for?' 'How can I better follow God in how I work and what I say?' Ultimately this is what 'God's will' is all about – living for Jesus every day. If you get that right, God promises to lead you every step of the way – and life's 'big decisions' will shrink down to merely the context in which you really do God's will.

6

Why isn't God Answering My Prayers?

Knowing that God is committed to sanctifying us in every circumstance gives us an amazing perspective on the decisions we have to make in life. You may agree with me that it is also unhelpful to think about options in terms of 'God's will' and 'not God's will'. But, at the end of the day, we still have to make these big decisions and we might wonder whether God has any preference or guidance for us. How do we go about discerning what that might be? Prayer is an obvious answer, but the reality is often not straightforward.

There have been occasions in my life when I've prayed and immediately known exactly what to do. There have even been situations where an idea has suddenly come into my mind, completely different from anything I was thinking about, and I was cautiously confident it was God's prompting. We believe in a supernatural God who can do all things and, although it is sensible to be cautious in pronouncing ideas in our heads as guidance from God, it is clear that God sometimes chooses to lead some people in this way. Nevertheless, while how much God communicates to us in this specific way is hard to tell, in my experience it is quite rare and we certainly shouldn't seek the prophetic voice of God at the expense of the Bible. As we shall examine in more detail later, God communicates to us through every line in the Bible and we should see Scripture as the primary means of hearing God.

What I have found to be more common, despite praying repeatedly and fervently, is the feeling that God is not answering. When we have a big decision to make, apparent silence from God can be incredibly frustrating. We can live in a place of uncertainty or confusion for weeks, months or even years at a time. If God isn't answering our cries for help, what should we do? I would think every Christian has experienced this – if you haven't, it may simply be because you've not been a Christian for long. We can take some, albeit small, comfort from the fact that this seems to be 'normal Christianity'.

But when our prayers seem to go unanswered, all sorts of doubts can creep into our minds. Have you had any of these thoughts? 'Maybe I'm not praying right … Maybe I'm not listening properly … Maybe because I've sinned this week God has turned away from me for a while … Maybe He isn't really there at all.'

Unfortunately, well-meaning Christian friends can even compound our frustration. We hear stories of other people's answers to prayer and direction from God, which came with apparent crystal clarity. Although we may try to be happy for them, inside we're crying out, 'God, why haven't You spoken to me?!'

As I have said, this is an experience common to all Christians. Furthermore, believe it or not, it can be a great place to be, even though it probably doesn't feel like it at the time. When we look beyond the fact that God is seemingly silent and think about the reasons *why*, we may actually come away encouraged. Let me explain three reasons for God's 'silence'.

1.God's silence grows our faith

When we don't feel that God is answering our prayers, we might well question His goodness and love for us. These doubts are temptations from the enemy (1 Thes. 3:5), who wants to disrupt our relationship with God and cause us to give up on trusting in Him. Yet the Bible is very clear that God loves us more than we can imagine and that in every circumstance He is working for our good. Best of all, God loves us not because of our good behaviour or in response to our obedience. Instead, He shows his love for us in that even though we were sinners, He sent His Son to die for us (Rom. 5:8), through whom we now stand before God as justified people. His love for us stretches from before we were even born to eternity (Eph. 1:4–5). So the idea that God might have turned away from us because we have sinned this week is foolish and a lie from 'the accuser' (Rev. 12:10). Nothing can separate us from God's love (Rom. 8:38–39). If God stopped loving anyone who sinned, then He wouldn't love any human at all, except Christ His Son.

As Christians we are assured of God's love for us. We can also be sure that God is always good. In fact God's goodness may be the reason that our prayers are seemingly unanswered right now. Have you ever considered that? God is a Father to us, and a good father knows what is best for his children. A father who immediately responds to every demand of their children is not a good father at all. Sometimes fathers have to say 'no' and sometimes they have to say 'wait'. That's not because they're mean; it's because they are more wise and loving than their children can even imagine. This difference in wisdom and love between a child and a father here on earth is infinitely smaller than that between us and our heavenly Father.

It may be the case that you're desperately praying for an answer from God. Have you stopped to consider that this in itself is a step in Christian maturity? An important part of growing as a Christian is developing deeper dependency on God. When God seems to withhold an answer from us, it could be because He wants us to exercise more faith and seek Him more eagerly for an answer.

The Bible says, 'pray continually' (1 Thes. 5:17). It doesn't say, 'Pray for a bit, but if it doesn't seem like things are going anywhere, just give up and try something else.' No, the very fact that Paul is encouraging this church to keep going is because the temptation to give up is often very strong. In other words, this verse makes sense only because God does not answer immediately after every prayer. Prayer is often a long-term pursuit – and it's no wonder we become frustrated if we treat it as a short-term solution.

When we were about to get married, my fiancée and I were looking for a flat to rent. We looked at a few places but they were awful and we were getting nowhere. Weeks went by and time began to run out. Then we even had one flat which we really liked snatched away from under our noses. As the summer went on – and with only a few weeks to go – my fiancée had to move back home to her parents' house while I stayed in Brighton to find somewhere.

All the way along this process we had been praying that God would provide but in all honesty I was also getting increasingly frustrated. I distinctly remember one day when I went into my bedroom, tired and irritated, and started really crying out to God in desperation. I wasn't politely asking God for something; I was fairly angry. I laid out to God in no uncertain terms the kind of flat I wanted, where it should be, how much we would pay for it and *demanded* that God supplied it within the next week or so. I had never prayed like that before, and in some ways it felt like I hadn't truly prayed until that day either.

It may sound like I wasn't being reverent, or perhaps you think that it is quite inappropriate to demand things from God when we are mere human beings. But I later realised that through this God was really teaching me how to wrestle in prayer. I had no right to be angry at God, but I'm so grateful He used the situation I was in to teach me a deeper lesson. If our faith is small, we might pray to begin with but we soon give up when God doesn't seem to answer. It takes more faith to persevere. It takes a strong faith to grab hold of God's promise to provide for us and to cry out to Him in desperation even when we're faced with His apparent silence and no change in the immediate circumstances. I demanded that God would answer because I felt I didn't have another option. God had to come through for us or we would be homeless newlyweds! As uncomfortable as being in that situation was at the time, being completely reliant on God is a great place to be.

And, of course, God did come through for us. A few days later we found a flat that fitted us just right. It wasn't exactly where I hoped it would be; it wasn't exactly what I'd asked for (it was a two-bed rather than a one-bed flat!); nor was it at the price I had in mind. But it was where God wanted us to be. The specifics of my prayer were less important than the fact that this episode in my life grew my faith and gave me new certainty about God's provision and the power of prayer. Many times since, when I've been praying about big things in life, I have remembered that time and it has caused me to be even bolder and perseverant in prayer.

God is not threatened by our demands. God is under no obligation to do exactly what we say, even though He dearly loves us. Ultimately what's best for us is to grow in our dependence on God and intimacy with Him. If that means God being silent for a while, that's what He'll do. God's silence is not an excuse to give up on prayer; it's actually an invitation to seek Him more vigorously. Maybe God is inviting you to seek Him with more of your heart (Jer. 29:13) and His silence is a doorway into that change in your life.

2. God's silence should drive us to what He has already said

We are extremely fortunate to live in a time and culture that has free access to God's Word. There are parts of the world today where people are not able to read the Bible. There have been numerous times in history, even since the formation of the Old and New Testaments, when barriers such as language and illiteracy have meant that only a select few people in society could read the Scriptures. We should not take for granted the free access we have to the eternal Truth of God's Word.

The fact is that every time we read a verse of Scripture, God is speaking to us. We need to take seriously that in each part of the Bible God is communicating to us. Therefore when we're faced with decisions in life, we shouldn't just ask God to give us an answer without also carefully considering what He has already said to us in the Bible. We've already seen that His Word is a lamp to our feet (Ps. 119:105).

The wrong way to do this is to treat the Bible as a 'magic book' that automatically tells us what to do in any given situation. As popular as it may be amongst immature Christians, opening the Bible on a random page and taking the first verse you see as God's message for you today is a very inappropriate way to treat God's Word. We need to be careful, not simplistic, about the way we interpret what the Bible says. For example, we should ask ourselves, what is the context? Who is it written to, for and about? Is the instruction or principle directly transferable to our situation? The Bible includes many different styles of literature and has many different original audiences in mind. While all of it is useful and relevant to us (2 Tim. 3:16–17), it is crucial to work out to whom God's words were originally spoken before we can draw any possible parallels to our lives. For instance, the Bible often tells us stories of sinful people who we should learn from as a warning, not view as an example to emulate. Certainly not all the Bible is prescriptive, so God is not necessarily telling us something we should do – let alone an answer to the particular situation in which we are – in every verse of the Bible.

However, often the Bible does have specific instructions that relate directly to situations we face. For example, in the run-up to a general election we may wonder who to vote for and be worried about what's going to happen in our country. 1 Timothy 2:1–2 informs us that we should pray for those who are in authority – we shouldn't worry; we should pray.

In other situations the Bible does not necessarily speak directly to the decision we face, but the general instruction it does give can help us make a good choice. Here's a hypothetical example to illustrate the point. A lady who's recently become a Christian is invited by a friend to a hen party. At this event she knows there will be male strippers and lots of sexual joking and conversation. Should she attend the party? She may pray about it and ask God for direction, but let's say for the sake of argument that God doesn't speak to her directly as she is praying. Does that mean that God is happy for her to go? Is that what God wants?

God's apparent silence to her prayers is not a 'green light' for her to attend the party, nor is it an indication that He doesn't have a strong opinion on the matter. The truth is that God has not been silent on this issue, even though this lady may not have 'heard' anything from God when she was praying. Ephesians 5:3–4 clearly speaks to this subject. I think we can conclude from it that attending this party would be inappropriate for someone who is following Jesus. Similarly 1 Corinthians 6:18 encourages us to 'flee' from sexual immorality, which to me suggests that we should be taking active steps in the opposite direction of it to avoid falling into temptation.

Another situation that is often debated amongst Christians is whether it is right or wrong for a Christian to marry someone who isn't a Christian. 2 Corinthians 6:14 speaks to the issue because Paul is warning the church not to partner themselves with those who don't share the faith, since Christ has made them radically different. If a member in my church came to me and said they were pursuing a relationship with someone who wasn't a Christian, they may try to assure me that they had prayed about it and, having heard no clear word from God to the contrary, felt peaceful that it was a good decision. However, I would point them to this verse and say that in fact God has already been sufficiently clear in the Bible.

Of course, some decisions that we have to make in our day-to-day lives are much more subtle than these. Nevertheless, the point still remains that in order to make good decisions in life, it is vitally important that we become familiar with what the Bible says. To repeat Psalm 119:105 again, 'Your word is a lamp for my feet, a light on my path.' When we search God's Word, it sheds light on our situation and makes things a lot clearer for us. Sometimes, especially if we are new to Christianity, we might not know what the Bible teaches about a particular topic, or where even to look in order to find out. That's why it's important to speak to trusted Christian friends and family about all sorts of decisions. The best advice they will give you is when they point you, lovingly and carefully, to what the Bible communicates.

There are some issues that certain Christians draw different conclusions on from others. There will be those who would draw different conclusions from the situations that I have described here. However, the most important thing is to submit our lives to God and His Word. With the access we have to God's Word, we have no excuse if we ask God for help simplistically, ignore what He has already put down in black and white for our instruction, and then as a result fall into temptation and sin. The Bible is of primary importance for us, whatever life decision we are trying to make.

3. God's silence may mean it's up to us

> *Do not conform to the pattern of this world, but be transformed by the renewing of your mind. Then you will be able to test and approve what God's will is – his good, pleasing and perfect will.*
> Romans 12:2

One of the great benefits of becoming familiar with the Bible is that we become shaped by its truth (Heb. 10:16). Though we are not always aware of it, we are constantly surrounded by a wide range of worldviews, opinions and attitudes that press in on us and vie for our attention and adoption. Though we may like to think of ourselves as independent freethinkers, the reality is that the instincts we have, the opinions and preferences we hold, and the knowledge and understanding we have gained is little more than a product of these outside influences. No child is born with wisdom or formed opinions. Over time their parents, siblings, friends, the media and a thousand other influences affect them and shape them into the people they grow up to be. We can be incredibly impressionable people and have a habit of soaking up the culture, beliefs and attitudes that are around us.

Not all of these influences are bad – many of them are extremely good – but if we can't help but be influenced by what we're exposed to, it is vital that we're exposed to the Bible as much as possible. The wisdom of the Bible is not just good advice for us to follow; it is a living book through which the Holy Spirit trains us in God's eternal wisdom.

As a consequence of this, it is sometimes not necessary or even appropriate to pray and ask God for an answer before we make certain decisions. God has given us a brain with decision-making capabilities; a measure of common sense (by His common grace); people around us to help; and the Bible. So we don't need to ask God whether we should put a seatbelt on when we're in a car – that's common sense. Nor do we need to ask God whether we should give to the poor – that's direct biblical instruction (Prov. 19:17). There will be many other decisions that God is happy for us to make in life without His specific intervention, even if they seem important to us.

When faced with decisions that are not so clear-cut, it is important that we seek God and pray about them. It's important that we do that in a persevering way, especially when there are big implications for us. It's also important that we become as informed as possible about the Bible's teaching and that we take on board advice from more mature Christians.

But if we have done all of that, and we are humble before God, it's entirely appropriate for us then to pick an option that we like. If we've heard no direct instruction from God, it could be that we're supposed to make the decision ourselves. We may never understand why God sometimes stays silent, but many, if not most, of the decisions we make will not be as a direct result of 'a word from God'.

When my wife and I were dating, I often prayed, 'God, should I marry her?' Quite understandably I wanted to know whether this relationship was right before God. For months on end I uttered that prayer, or variations of it, but I never felt I received an answer from Him. I knew that continuing to go out with her with no plan to marry would be wrong – that's not the way the Bible presents romantic relationships. (See my book *First* for more on that.) But I didn't get any sense that God was saying, 'Yes, ask her to marry you.' What I realised was that in this instance God wanted me to make a decision. Marrying her was my choice, and a choice that I would need to stick to for the rest of my life. Was I ready for that? Is that something I wanted to do? That was for me to answer.

Sometimes we ask God for an answer because we're scared of making a decision for ourselves. I wanted God to confirm things for me so that the decision would be less daunting. But getting married is daunting! We're supposed to be anxious about our choice because it's one of the most important decisions in life.

Being a Christian does not mean that every big decision has to be a 'word from God'. Don't be paralysed by silence. If you're humble before Him and submit your life to His ways, you really won't go far wrong.

But what if you do go wrong? Let's discuss that in the next chapter.

7

What if I Mess Up My Life?

Maybe you've recently become a Christian and you're turning to God because you realise your life is a bit of a mess. Maybe you just don't know what to do with your life and you've gone from one thing to another, with nothing really working out. The good news is that God is an expert at making great stories out of seemingly hopeless situations. However badly we feel we've messed things up, or even if we just have no idea where we're headed, with God there's always real hope for the future. Sometimes we feel where we've ended up can't possibly be part of His good plan for our lives, but God loves taking us on a journey that may seem unexpected to us yet ultimately is full of His blessing. Let me remind you of Romans 8:28: 'And we know that in all things God works for the good of those who love him, who have been called according to his purpose.'

God loves us and therefore He's working for our good. Notice it says, 'in all things'. Yes, in your situation too! An example from the Bible is the story of Joseph (Gen. 37–50). Joseph was the victim of circumstances that he didn't deserve. If we had met him at several points in his life, we really wouldn't have thought God was working much good in his life at all. But when we look at the big picture, we realise what an expert plan God was accomplishing.

The story begins with Joseph as a young man. He is his father's favourite and is given an ornate robe, which antagonises his brothers. Then he has some prophetic dreams about his brothers bowing down to him, which increases his brothers' hatred towards him. As a result, his brothers plot to kill him. Though he avoids death, he is sold into slavery.

If something like this happened to you or me, we would probably worry that we had missed God's will for our life. Slavery doesn't sound something a loving God would want for His child, does it? Maybe you've found yourself in a job or situation that's just awful. How did you respond?

It is easy to pray, 'God, get me out of here!' Sometimes, though, a better prayer is, 'God, what do you want to do in my life?' As I've already said,

God's priority is us becoming more like Him, and we see from numerous stories in the Bible that God isn't afraid to use temporary hardship to bring about this. Difficulty in life is sometimes what God utilises to grow us into the people He wants us to be. It's not the only way God does so, but any mature Christian will tell you that it is an important one. God uses every step of our lives to work for our good. In Joseph's situation God used the hardship of slavery to position him for the next chapter in his life.

Joseph is taken to the foreign land of Egypt where he serves as a slave to Potiphar, one of Pharaoh's officials. Eventually he is given more and more responsibility. I think it's safe to conclude that his godly attitude aided this series of promotions. It's important to remember that even when we are in difficult situations or a job we don't like or feel has been a bad choice, God still wants us to live and work as if we are doing so for Him (Eph. 6:7). God wants us to follow Him at all times, not just when we feel we've found our calling in life.

After gaining a position of great responsibility as Potiphar's right-hand man, Joseph's life again takes a tumble – not due to an error on his part but *because* he makes a good and godly decision. Joseph finds himself in a place of temptation when Potiphar's wife tries to seduce him. What does he do? He runs! But this decision sees him end up in jail because Potiphar's wife lies about the incident and puts the blame all on him.

Again, take a moment to reflect on this. Just because we choose to follow God doesn't mean things will go swimmingly for us. Sometimes, as here with Joseph, we immediately hit opposition. We shouldn't be surprised if putting God first actually brings suffering into our lives. Joseph ends up in some unexpected places, many of them very bad, but God is bigger than his suffering and is still working for his good, weaving an incredible story in his life. It is the same for us.

At this point it might be helpful for me to point out that there are some Christians who suggest that because of what Jesus has done for us, we can expect comfort and prosperity for the rest of our lives. This so-called Christian teaching is sometimes called the 'prosperity gospel'. While I do not want to go into this in detail here, it is important to understand that God never promises us prosperity in this world – our lives will not be perfect until we are with Him in His new creation. Yes, God does promise us blessing now, and He even invites us to trust Him for particular blessings in our lives such as material possessions (2 Cor. 9:10; Phil. 4:19; Mal. 3:10; Mark 10:29–30). Therefore, there is nothing wrong with asking God to cause your career to be a success or even for you to be blessed financially. But of the many problems with the 'prosperity gospel', one of the main ones is that it refuses to acknowledge that God has the right to say 'no.'

Sometimes God will say 'no' to our comfort and material gain, even if it is just for a short while, to accomplish a greater work in us, which is far more important – his priority of our sanctification (1 Thes. 4:3).

He loves to bless us in all sorts of ways because He is the best possible father (Matt. 7:11). But, as I have already said, any father who says 'yes' to every request of his children is not a good father at all. A wise father understands that saying 'no' is sometimes the best way to love because what he wants to give is even better than what his children are asking for. For example, God might say 'no' to us having wealth in order to say 'yes' to us learning humility, patience and faith. Such instances should neither surprise us nor cause us to doubt God. In contrast, if someone thinks material prosperity is the best thing God can do for them and sees Him simply as a means to achieve this, I'd wonder whether their heart has been changed by the Gospel at all.

God certainly didn't say 'yes' to Joseph enjoying comfort. Years spent in slavery and prison must have been extremely tough for him. He must have wondered what God was doing. How could this possibly be God's plan? But Joseph couldn't have even imagined the heights to which God would take him next. Through miraculous circumstances Joseph is raised up to be prime minister of all Egypt. He eventually saves the nation, including his brothers who betrayed him, from famine and brings God's rich blessing on them all. It's an incredible story – you really should read it.

God can use any and every circumstance and decision we make to bring about His plan for our lives. Our weaknesses, failures, bad decisions and mistakes do not place us outside of God's purposes. Near the end of his life, Joseph speaks to his brothers and reflects on how God has woven His plan through all of their decisions. He reassures them with these amazing words: 'You intended to harm me, but God intended it for good to accomplish what is now being done, the saving of many lives' (Gen. 50:20).

What an amazing God! He takes even the evil that is perpetrated and turns it into a story of incredible blessing for many, many people. We should understand that God was achieving his great salvation plan through Joseph – it was a particular time and place in Bible history. We must be wary of expecting the same remarkable outcome. Nevertheless, we can learn lessons from the life of Joseph. Whether we feel we're in the pit or are just at the beginning of our adventure with God and are worried about where it might lead, God is committed to weaving an amazing story with our lives. Even though it will include many ups and downs, it will also be of immense blessing to us and many others.

Part Three:
Wisdom for the Real World

8

Entertainment

We live in an age of entertainment. No generation before us has enjoyed the comfort, technology and access to entertainment that we currently have – and it's brilliant. What a rich and diverse feast of creativity and talent is at our fingertips! Someone can write a song on the other side of the world and within minutes we can be enjoying it in our homes or on the bus or in the park. We can watch a multi-million-dollar American television series as we sit on the toilet! What a world we live in.

Everything that is good about music, television, film and all other types of entertainment is from God (Ps. 24:1). It is a reflection of His goodness and part of His creative flair (Ps. 19:1). The acting that grips us, the music that moves us, the talent that wows us and even the technology that astounds us all find their source in God (John 1:3). He has made an incredible world and incredible people with incredible gifts, and it is our privilege, given to us by God, to enjoy it. Acknowledging this should be the foundation of a Christian attitude to entertainment. We should thank God for it every day, along with the many other blessings that we receive from Him (1 Tim. 4:4–5). Many Christians 'say grace' before a meal, but it would be equally good and right to do the same before we watch a film or listen to an album. It's important to regularly acknowledge that all good things come from God.

In fact failing to thank God for the good things that He has blessed us with is the first step in sliding away from a relationship with God. The curse of sin that has affected all of humanity has its roots in ungratefulness (Rom. 1:21). Instead of turning to God in praise and thanks as a natural response to His amazing creation – whether we are enthralled by a sunset or mesmerised by a movie – we sinful humans generally have taken it for granted.

We're not grateful because we sinfully assume that creation is here to serve us, rather than realising that we are here to serve God. We think this is a wise conclusion to make, but God says it is utter foolishness (Rom. 1:22). That's not to say science is foolishness. Science is all about understanding creation and that's an amazing pursuit. But the key question is, how do our hearts respond to what we see in life? Do we marvel at and praise the creation itself or do we lift our heads in response to creation to the Creator who sits above it? The Bible's definition of foolishness is not whether someone is clever or not, but whether someone refuses to acknowledge God as the Creator of all things.

Paul, in the first chapter of Romans, continues to diagnose the predicament of humankind by underlining that we not only have refused to acknowledge and worship God, but we've decided to worship creation itself instead (v. 23)! When the Bible talks about 'idols', we might think of metal or wooden statues, shrines and temples. However, idolatry certainly includes but is not limited to these pagan rituals. People give their utter devotion to many things, whether they fully realise it or not. Today people worship the 'gods' of career success, sexual freedom, alcohol, food, diet, body image, Premier League football – the list is endless! It may seem over the top to describe these things as idols, but people's attitude towards them is the key indicator of what is really going wrong in their hearts. Often people trust in these things to make them happy. What may start off as a casual interest can become more and more controlling until people begin to shape their lives around it. When people pursue these things relentlessly, despite the great costs that they may incur as a result, they have unwittingly succumbed to idolatry.

Entertainment is one such potential idol in

our society. While entertainment is intrinsically good, it's important that Christians are aware of its power. In a society that is obsessed with entertainment, it is sometimes difficult not to get carried away by everyone else, adopting similar attitudes and spending inordinate amounts of time and money on it. Just the sheer quantity as well as the quality of it makes it particularly dangerous. In generations gone by there were less than a handful of television channels and they didn't even screen programmes all day! Today you could literally watch TV endlessly, not just on the hundreds of channels available but also from DVD box sets and instant streaming services. Almost any film that you can think of is available to you at the touch of a button.

Let me emphasise again that today's wealth of entertainment is a privileged and blessed situation. But with such a great feast set out before us, gluttony is a real danger. Therefore, while it is good and right that we should enjoy entertainment and thank God for it, every Christian should regularly consider the amount of time they give to it and reflect on whether it is appropriate.

How much time should Christians spend on entertainment?

Relaxation and recreation are not just nice things to have in life; they are a biblically commanded (Ex. 34:21). Of course, in the new covenant that Jesus has inaugurated we Christians are not bound by the Old Testament laws – including those concerning the Sabbath. Nevertheless, the principle of rest is one that God has clearly built into creation (Gen. 2:2) and so to ignore it would be unwise. The reality is we are finite human beings who are made to work but cannot keep going and going indefinitely. Enjoying God's creative gifts is good and beneficial in helping us to unwind and relax.

Where entertainment can become a problem is if we go beyond this principle and it becomes a distraction from the rest of our lives. Perhaps we simply watch things for the sake of it. As I have already mentioned, the potential for this is open to us more than ever before. Few people watch a TV series one episode at a time anymore – the term 'binge-watch' is now in the dictionary for a reason. If you're streaming a series online, without you even pressing a button the next episode will automatically begin. Another forty minutes of television can easily slip by.

I don't want to make anyone feel guilty for simply watching box sets – my wife and I watch them quite a lot. But, like so many aspects of life, we should regularly reflect upon how we are honouring God with our time. Do we have an appropriate balance? God has called us to many things in life including work (Gen. 2:15), serving others (Gal. 5:13), being generous (2 Cor. 9:6–7), providing for our families (1 Tim. 5:8), sharing the Gospel (2 Cor. 5:18–21) and deepening our relationship with God through studying His Word (Ps. 1:1–2) and prayer (Luke 18:1). In light of this we should consider how much of our lives we give to entertainment. We must also have our eyes open to the fact that the devil wants to distract us from all that God has called us to do – Satan's very happy for us to be sitting on the sofa for hours if it causes us to neglect these things.

So how much is too much? As you may expect, I am not going to make specific recommendations. The answer will have different answers for different people in different circumstances. Someone who is sick in hospital may have little else to do than spend a few hours watching films and it distracts them from their pain. But a husband with several children and a demanding job may well be shunning his God-given responsibilities if he sits in front of the screen for hours every day. Each one of us should carefully consider for ourselves how much time we should give to enjoying entertainment. The point is that we should consider it. If we don't, it's very easy to get swept along with the consumerist entertainment culture that we are in. We are called to something greater than that.

It's worth adding that all forms of entertainment are given for us to enjoy and – with some exceptions that we will look at next – one is not more 'holy' than another. I'm sometimes surprised how certain Christians may look down their noses at others in the church who play computer games but will happily spend the same amount of time reading novels. We're called to love God, enjoy Him and serve Him. The right amount of entertainment in our lives can help us do this but the wrong amount has the potential to distract us from this call.

What forms of entertainment are off limits to a Christian?

So far we have largely focused on the time we spend enjoying entertainment. We need to consider what we watch and listen to as well. However long you have been a Christian, you will have some instincts about what is and isn't appropriate to watch, but our conscience isn't the only thing that should guide us in this area.

Some things are more clear-cut than others. For example, most Christians would not need much convincing that watching pornography is not something God wants us to do. The Bible frequently encourages us to run in the opposite direction to sexually immorality (1 Cor. 6:18) and Jesus shocks His disciples by saying that lust is the equivalent of breaking God's commandment about adultery (Matt. 5:28). God is concerned with what goes on in our minds concerning sexual purity, not just what we do with our bodies.

The more subtle question is whether Christians should watch films or TV series, play computer games or listen to music that contain, for example, some level of sexual content, bad language or violence. Where do we draw the line? If it's two minutes of inappropriate content in a two-hour film, does it really matter? If there are a few swear words here and there in a song, is it wrong to listen to it? Is watching violence an issue? There's plenty of violence in the Bible, after all!

These are important questions. As with the previous discussion, it is not helpful for me to give specific instruction in this area. First, because the Bible does not speak directly to the issue, so we must be cautious about drawing fixed conclusions where God has not done so. Second, because God allows and encourages us to exercise a level of personal judgement and conscience-informed decision-making (Rom. 14:1–4). Third, being honest, because I'm not completely sure of the answers myself!

Having said that, there are some biblical principles that help us to make good decisions in this area. First, verses such as 1 Corinthians 6:18 and Matthew 5:28 give us a clear indication that God cares about what we expose ourselves to, particularly when it comes to sexual behaviour. It is worth pointing out that the New Testament authors did not have modern films in mind when they wrote these words. They are most directly referring to the practice of sexual immorality – engaging in sexual behaviour with people we are not married to. Modern readers might point out that simply watching behaviour on screen is very different to doing it yourself, but it is not as different as we might think. Who can watch sexual behaviour and not be tempted to fantasise themselves? It is possible, but we have to admit that in doing so we are opening the door to the temptation of lust that Jesus talks so directly about. Is that wise? We mustn't treat it as unimportant.

Second, there is a clear biblical principle of sowing and reaping that is relevant to this discussion. I think this can help us to consider the violence, profanity, horror, witchcraft, sexual content and more generally the powerful but ungodly attitudes and worldviews that music, television and films communicate to us. Galatians 6:8 declares, 'Whoever sows to please their flesh, from the flesh will reap destruction; whoever sows to please the Spirit, from the Spirit will reap eternal life.'

This verse is primarily about salvation and the eternal consequences of our decision to accept Christ or live in 'the flesh' – a phrase often used in the Bible to refer to a purely physical or 'worldly' existence. The implication is that when we come to Christ, our attitude to life will fundamentally change. What is appropriate to invest, or sow, into becomes completely different than when our 'flesh' was our primary concern. But the reality is we're still undergoing this process of change and part of us still gravitates towards a worldly existence. The Christian therefore has to make daily decisions about how they will 'sow' and what they will 'reap'.

In other words, what we expose our lives to can feed our sinful nature that is at odds with following Christ. If we spend a lot of time listening to music that's full of swearing, we will likely become more tempted to swear ourselves. When we watch television programmes about rich people who enjoy great wealth and luxury, it can unhelpfully fuel jealousy in our lives. Films that objectify women or men in a sexual way can affect our thoughts and attitudes too, often in subtle ways that build up over time. I'm not saying that watching sinful behaviour causes us to sin, but no-one is immune from being influenced – we're much more impressionable than we like to believe. We mustn't be naive about the dangers and power of temptation (1 Pet. 5:8). We should also be aware that some temptations are more powerful over us than others. Watching a film with sex and gore may be fascinating for all the wrong reasons to a teenager, and a television show about houses may fuel the temptation of jealousy and discontent for a middle-aged person.

If ever a Christian comes to me about a sinful habit they are struggling to break, I will make sure to question carefully with what they are filling their mind day by day. How can anyone hope to reap the fruit of the Spirit, which includes self-control, when they spend all their time sowing to the flesh? We reap what we sow in our lives. We mustn't fool ourselves into thinking that what we watch or listen to or engage in has no effect on our lives.

Filling our thoughts and minds with sex or gore or ungodly attitudes can be a hindrance to developing the godly behaviour and attitudes that God calls us to.

Yes, because Jesus has saved us, there is freedom. There is no law against watching the latest TV box set or Oscar-tipped film. But Paul warns the Corinthians that although everything is permissible, not everything is helpful (1 Cor. 10:23). He tells the Ephesians, after warning them against all sorts of ungodly behaviour, 'Live as children of light' (Eph. 5:8) and he instructs the Colossians, 'Set your minds on things above, not on earthly things' (Col. 3:2). These verses should give us suitable caution when considering what we should listen to or watch.

Before I close this chapter let me give a brief example from my own life, not because I am saying 'do as I do' but because I know practical details are helpful, even just as a reference point. There are very few films rated '18' that I would watch. There are some I have and, with hindsight, should probably not have done. There are some '15's that I have seen that were not helpful for me at all and I know I shouldn't watch again. I don't want to pin God's instruction to some man-made and changeable rating system, but this may help you to think for yourself about what is appropriate and what is not. Besides, with the wealth of television and films available to us, there's always something else to watch!

Another overarching principle that I find helpful is whether I can 'say grace' – as I would before enjoying a meal – before watching a particular film or television show, playing a certain computer game, reading a specific article or book, or listening to an album. That thought process helps me to consider whether I really can enjoy something as a blessing from God with a thankful heart.

Of course, all forms of entertainment are marred by sin. We can't live in this world without being exposed to ungodly content. But to some extent we can tolerate sin without it having a negative effect on our lives. The problem is when engaging in entertainment will cause us to sin in thought, word or deed. When we honestly ask ourselves my question, we may realise it's inappropriate to 'say grace' for it and therefore we should refrain from it. But if we can enjoy it as a good gift from God rather than a selfish indulgence, then we are free to do so with thanksgiving.

9

Money

One thing students look forward to after university is the prospect of earning some money. Having mainly lived off loans or borrowed money, meaning their disposable income was quite limited, the prospect of earning a wage each month and having some money to spend is a particularly welcome one. But when you've got some money in your pocket, what should you do with it? How should being a Christian shape your financial behaviour?

These are important questions to ask, whether you've just graduated or have recently become a Christian, particularly because money is one of the topics Jesus most frequently discussed in his earthly ministry. Flick through the Gospels and it won't be long before you find a passage where

Jesus is challenging His hearers about their attitude towards money. That may surprise you – surely Jesus' main priority would be to talk about salvation, forgiveness and God's character? Of course all of those things were key parts of His ministry, but He also kept coming back to the subject of money. Why? It was because money is one of the key pillars of society and affects most aspects of the lives we lead. If you have it, a world of opportunities is open to you. If you don't have it, just surviving day to day is a challenge. What's more, few subjects reveal the attitude of our hearts like money does. Look at someone's bank statement – what they choose to spend their money on, what sacrifices they choose to make and what generosity they choose to show – and you'll get a good picture of their priorities in life. What does yours say about you?

Understandably many of us think about money a lot of the time: 'Do I have enough? … What can I afford? … What will I spend my next pay cheque on? … What would it be like to have more?' In Jesus' day, I'm sure, these questions occupied people just as much as they do today.

So what does He have to say *to us* about this important subject? A foundational truth is that *our* money is not completely ours. This can be extremely challenging to us, especially at first, because as we earn money, of course we have an instinctive sense that our income belongs to us. But can we take *all* the credit for it? We might be in possession of it, but who made money in the first place?

The Bible says that all of creation was made by Jesus and for Jesus (Col. 1:16). If we earn or simply receive something, that doesn't mean it's any less His. We may own the clothes that we wear, but they are also part of God's creation and ultimately belong to Him. Likewise, the money we earn is both ours and God's. 'The earth is the LORD's, and everything in it,' says Psalm 24:1, but God has also given humanity the clear role of looking after it on His behalf (Gen. 1:28). So we can receive our salary from our employer and at the same time acknowledge that it also comes from God's hand and is a gift from Him. Since it is a gift, it really does belong to us – it wouldn't be much of a gift if we didn't have any sense of real ownership over it. But our wage doesn't stop being His just because it's moved into a bank account with our name on it.

We should receive our income in a similar way to how we receive all the other good things in God's creation, such as food, laughter and sunny days – as blessings we can enjoy from our loving heavenly Father. He wants us to thank Him for them, enjoy them, steward them with wisdom and share them generously with others.

How to give

We have the foundational principle, but what does it look like in practice? How do we honour God and get the right balance of enjoying money for ourselves now, stewarding it wisely for the future and being generous in giving too?

Let me address giving first and spending second because I believe the Bible puts them in that order. That's not to say that we should necessarily give more than we spend, but the principle of generosity takes its place ahead of self-interest for the Christian. A memorable phrase that I have found extremely helpful is, 'Give to God what's right, not what's left.' I think this summarises much of the Bible's teaching on the subject very well.

If we want to follow Jesus, giving is a non-negotiable. When Jesus talked about it, He said, 'when you give', not 'if you give' (Matt. 6:3). We're told that 'God loves a cheerful giver' (2 Cor. 9:7) and instructed to prioritise His kingdom (Matt. 6:25–34). When the 'rich young ruler' thought he had done all that God required of him, Jesus challenged him to give away all he had (Mark 10:17–27). Like this man, we might hear Jesus' words and come away discouraged that God would require so much of us. These are difficult teachings indeed!

But this reaction isn't that surprising when we reflect upon our sinful nature. Without God in our lives, our natural instinct is to look after number one. We believe that what we can gain in terms of material and financial riches will help us in the ultimate pursuit of serving ourselves. This is the way we have been hardwired under the curse of sin. That's not to say we have to become Christians in order to be charitable or generous – of course we don't – but without God your life story is in the end just about you, and the instinct towards selfishness will likely be what largely shapes decisions.

When we meet Jesus, we realise that God made us and wants us to be part of His big story. We were made to love and live for Him. Life isn't about what we can gain or earn; it's about following Jesus. This is why Jesus urges us to not be anxious about life but seek first His kingdom (Matt. 6:25–34). When life is just about me, it's very hard not to worry: 'Am I being successful enough? ... Do I have enough money? ... What can I buy? ... What shall I wear? ... What if I lose my job?' We naturally trust in ourselves for even the basic provision we need to survive. Jesus instead invites us to prioritise Him and trust that He will look after us.

In monetary terms, seeking first His kingdom means, primarily, giving to the poor and giving to gospel work. Giving to churches and mission organisations is an obvious application of 'God's kingdom' but looking after the poor in society, whether directly connected with evangelism or not, also seems to be a 'kingdom theme' that runs right through the Bible (Prov. 19:17; Acts 2:45; Gal. 2:10).

How much should we give, then? In the Old Testament God was quite specific about what giving should look like. God's people were required to tithe, meaning a tenth of their income or wealth should be contributed towards the temple. Should Christians continue with this principle and give a tenth of their income? I would say that tithing is a great place to start if you've not given before. You will find giving away ten per cent of what you receive a challenging and counter-cultural step of faith. It may be a big sacrifice for you and mean that you will have to make tough financial decisions in order to make it happen. For others tithing is a first step that can helpfully lead into bigger proportional giving.

However, as helpful as the principle of tithing is, this instruction was given as part of the old covenant law. God's people now relate to Him through the new covenant of grace that we experience through Jesus. The New Testament emphasis is one of generosity in giving rather than a legalistic requirement (2 Cor. 9:6).

There are many other verses that can help inform our decisions when it comes to giving. First, as I've already said, giving is not an optional extra for a Christian or something that comes with 'maturity' but should be a practice from day one (Matt. 6:3). When we give, we express trust in God and fulfil a role as a channel of God's blessing to the world (Matt. 10:8).

Second, regular giving should be the norm; our giving shouldn't be sporadic. If it's a priority in our lives, then we should be intentional about it. New

Testament churches were instructed to set money aside each week (1 Cor. 16:2) in order to give to missionary work and support churches. We're called to be generous, but that doesn't mean we have to 'feel inspired' every time we give. Churches and organisations are wonderfully blessed when we commit our giving to them in an intentional and long-term way by using direct debits or similar systems. If our giving is to reflect God's giving to us (Luke 6:38; Matt. 10:8), then we must recognise that God has given to us in an intentional and committed way that doesn't in any way change according to mood (Rom. 8:32).

Third, 1 Corinthians 16:2 also teaches that our giving should be proportional to our income. The Bible has two primary emphases with regards money: generosity (1 Tim. 6:18) and stewardship (Luke 12:48). Stewardship involves being wise with our finances but we should not see it as an alternative to giving or think that the two are in competition with each other. Generosity can be misapplied as just sporadic giving, and stewardship can be misapplied as an excuse to be overcautious. The reality is that God calls us to be both generous and good stewards, and we should pursue both in our walk with Jesus. It doesn't honour God to overstretch ourselves financially and get into difficulty, but we can give proportionally in a faith-filled way – by planning carefully while at the same time asking God regularly to speak to us and guide us about how and when we should give. Likewise, making medium- or long-term giving commitments is a good thing to do but should not prevent us from giving cheerfully in a spur-of-the-moment, short-term way too (2 Cor. 9:7)

Fourth, and related to this, we should give gladly and not out of any sense of guilt. The Bible underlines that compulsion is completely the wrong motivation for giving (2 Cor. 9:7). Instead, it is important that we pray and decide in our hearts the right amount to give. Giving should be a heartfelt response of worship, gratitude and love to the God who has been overwhelmingly generous to us in giving His Son (Rom. 8:32).

To conclude this section, giving is not a legalistic requirement. The Gospel has brought us into complete freedom (Gal. 5:13) and this includes in the area of money. We are not enslaved to the pursuit of money because, unlike the world, we do not see it as our 'security'. We are free to bless others through generous giving because we have already been the greatest recipients of generosity anyone could experience. And we can freely pursue putting God's kingdom first and taking steps of faith in our giving knowing that God has promised to look after us and provide everything we need.

How to spend

If giving is to be a priority in our lives, how should this affect the way we spend on ourselves? This is a huge question that has been answered by Christians in many different ways. Some have suggested that a Christian life should be one of simplicity to the point of poverty and an almost complete rejection of material possessions and wealth. At the other extreme there are so-called Christians who suggest that overwhelming financial prosperity is a direct outworking of the Gospel and something that every Christian can achieve.

Despite being quite prevalent in the world today – though thankfully not as much in this country as elsewhere – the second example is profoundly wrong. Greed is not a virtue and it is a perversion of the gospel message to suggest that Jesus died on the cross to make us rich. Much more could be said on this matter, but the Bible speaks clearly and definitively on it: 'Those who want to get rich fall into temptation and a trap and into many foolish and harmful desires that plunge people into ruin and destruction' (1 Tim. 6:9).

The first example, the pursuit of poverty, also makes a mistake by seeing finances and possessions as an obstacle to a spiritually fruitful life. As I have explained before, all the things that we have, including the money in our bank accounts, are good gifts from God for us to enjoy (1 Tim. 6:17). We should receive them with thanksgiving, not treat them as always a stone in the road to trip us up.

Although Jesus has something to say to the wealthy in society (1 Tim. 6:17–19), His instruction is not to become poor. If God has given us money, it's not necessarily wrong to buy things for ourselves, even expensive things like nice holidays, gadgets, cars, meals or whatever else we like to enjoy. Yes, God's people are to be channels of His blessing (Deut. 28:12) but we are also free to be recipients of His blessing too. Whether you have great wealth or little wealth, enjoy it! We shouldn't feel guilty about being blessed by God.

As with most things, God is primarily concerned with the attitude of our hearts more than how much things cost or which items end up in our shopping bags (Luke 16:13–15). He calls us to enjoy and be grateful for the blessing of good things in life. He also calls us be a blessing, not being selfish but remembering the poor (Gal. 2:10). He calls us to support gospel work in a committed way. He calls us to have an eternal perspective, prioritising and investing in the kingdom of heaven.

We're called to all of these things and so we must prayerfully and wisely seek to balance them in our lives. Money is good but the love of money is a root to evil (1 Tim. 6:10). Being rich isn't wrong but desiring to be rich is a sinful temptation. These teachings are subtle and often difficult to know how to apply. No wonder Jesus spoke so much about the subject of money. We need the ongoing help of His Spirit if we're going to do well in this area of our lives. The reality is there is no simple solution or financial strategy that best honours God. Over the years my spending, saving and giving have gone up and down as circumstances have changed and God has challenged me and taught me in different ways. It is an adventure that requires faith and trust. It is not an easy one but certainly a sanctifying one if we submit this area of our lives completely to Him.

10

Clothes

How does being a Christian affect what we wear?
Maybe that's not a question you regularly ask
yourself but it's probably more important than you
realise. Whether we like it or not, what we wear is
a form of communication. Through the clothing
we choose we're sending and receiving messages
all the time. When someone walks into a room, it's
almost impossible to not make judgements about
what they are like based on what they wear. We
might not intend to do this, or even realise that we
are, but, rightly or wrongly, we pick up impressions
and signals from the way people present themselves.
We don't have to wear something crazy to 'make
a statement'; whether we're dressing fashionably,
boringly or anything in between, we're making

them all the time with the way we dress.

Some Christians are really into fashion whereas others couldn't care less; both are absolutely fine. Fashion can be enjoyed as a gift from God just like any other interest or hobby that we might have. But what we wear is something that we all need to think about. God cares about how we present ourselves and particularly the motives in our hearts for our decisions. The topic of modesty is mentioned several times in the Bible (1 Tim. 2:9–10; 1 Pet. 3:3–4; Prov. 11:22; 1 Pet. 5:5; Matt. 6:1; 1 Tim. 4:12). Despite this it's not something that gets talked about very much, in my experience. I have never heard a sermon about it in my churchgoing life. Yet since we dress ourselves every day (at least I hope we do!), it's important that we're informed on what God has to say about modesty. This isn't a topic for women alone either; we all need to think this one through.

Before I launch into some practical considerations about dressing modestly, let me put it in context by asking another question you may never have even thought about: why do we wear clothes at all? Again, the answer is more important and Gospel-centred than you might realise and actually helpful to the decisions we have to make in this area.

If you know your Bible, you'll know that the first humans didn't wear clothes (Gen. 2:25). Yes, the Bible begins with nudity, but it doesn't stay that way for long. When Adam and Eve turned away from

God and sinned, their lack of clothes sadly became a source of shame to them (Gen. 3:10). Amazingly, God Himself therefore provided clothes for them (Gen. 3:21), which is a picture of the covering of our sin and shame that comes ultimately through Jesus. On the first pages of the Bible, then, we see a direct link between nudity, shame and sin. The fact that people in society (in general) wear clothes is not just an accident or a matter of preference or convenience. There is something inherently shameful and vulnerable in our eyes about nudity that strikes at the heart of who we are as fallen human beings.

As a result of this, attempts to uncover what should be covered is not just 'a bit rude'; it's attempting to reject the idea that humankind is fallen and sinful. The vulnerability we feel and our need to be covered actually point to our need for our sins to be 'covered' at the cross. Contrary to the paintings and statues you might have seen, the Bible describes Jesus as being naked on the cross (John 19:23). He took our sin and He took our shame by becoming sinful and shameful as He died in our place. Who knew the Gospel had so much to do with nudity?

Pursuing modesty

This context helps us to see that the Bible's instructions about modesty are not just rules based in the cultural values of the time. Nor should the modern Christian view of clothes have its roots in prudish, Victorian attitudes. No, modesty's importance lies in the fundamental relationship between God and humankind as described at the beginning of Scripture.

This perspective is radically different from that of our society in general. We live in a time and culture where there is an ongoing fascination with all that should be 'hidden', and this is not surprising. The reason that sex and nudity are so powerful and fascinating to us is precisely because they are illicit. Our God-given instinct knows that they should be 'covered' and 'hidden', until they find their appropriate, God-defined context, but our selfish and sinful instinct wants to grab hold of that which is 'forbidden'. It is the same instinct that caused Adam and Eve to take hold of the fruit of the tree of life (Gen. 3:6).

But what difference does that make to the clothing decisions we make each day? Although few readers will be struggling with the urge to walk down the street naked, many, if not most, will be tempted to follow at least general trends in fashion. We must think carefully about which of these to embrace and which to reject.

Our understanding of the 'theology of clothes' is important because it helps us to understand the great difference between the Christian's perspective and that of the world's fashion houses. The sinful instinct to expose what should be hidden can be summed up, more or less, in what the world calls 'sexy'. This pursuit of 'sexiness' does not run through all fashion – I'm not saying that – but it is certainly a dominant theme and most of the time this is in direct contradiction to the Bible's dominant theme of modesty. We can't pursue 'sexiness', self-interest or self-promotion at the same time as prioritising humility and modesty (Rom. 12:3). 1 Timothy 2:9 expresses it this way: 'I also want the women to dress modestly, with decency and propriety, adorning themselves, not with elaborate hairstyles or gold or pearls or expensive clothes'.

The idea behind being 'sexy' is to declare, 'Look at me.' Let me repeat that I am not just talking about women here; this applies to both genders. It is the design, through physical appearance, to gain the attention of others, most particularly sexually charged attention. It is a self-promotion, tempting others to fantasise about you. This effect is, of course, best achieved by exposing, or tempting to expose, what should be hidden and private. I don't have to go into detail here – you know what I mean.

This attitude is the exact opposite of what Paul describes by the term 'modestly' in 1 Timothy 2:9. Christian women – and I would argue that this applies to men too, maybe now even more than in Paul's day – should not seek to attract attention to themselves through their clothes. 'Sexiness' should not be pursued, but modesty should be the shaping concern for a Christian when dressing themselves.

Thus modesty should inform our decisions when buying clothes and getting dressed. Which clothes allow us to preserve and pursue modesty, and which are about sexual suggestion or self-promotion? I challenge you to ask Christian friends of the opposite sex what type of clothes attract their attention in an unhelpful way. It could be anything from low-cut tops, to short skirts or shorts, to T-shirts that accentuate muscles or a toned physique! What attention do your clothes receive and what is your agenda for wearing them?

Unfortunately, many Christians, because they haven't really considered what these Bible verses mean, blindly follow the pattern set by high-street stores and dress 'sexily'. Others, though maybe more aware of the issues, ask themselves, 'What can I get away with as a Christian?' I do not want to sound unduly judgemental and harsh here – if I am honest, I have asked myself that question too. I have chosen to think the way the world thinks rather than to bring Jesus into this decision. I want to be sexy too! Even if we're not consciously going through that thought process, it's so easy to get caught up in this attitude and wonder how far we can 'push the boundaries' of appropriate attire.

But, like so many things in the Christian life, if we're wondering how far we can push the boundaries of what the Bible says, we're in completely the wrong place. We shouldn't be asking ourselves, 'What can I get away with?' We should be asking ourselves, 'Am I pursuing modesty?' Paul describes modesty as something to pursue here, not a concession to make. This radical attitude should completely change the conversation from, 'Are these shorts too short?' or 'Is this top too low?' to abandoning the pursuit of self-glorification and seeking to honour God as much as possible (1 Cor. 10:31).

Having said this applies to both men and women, I do realise it is practically more difficult for women – I don't envy their task of finding suitable modest clothing considering what is on offer in high-street stores. But the narrow road of following Christ is rarely easy and our wardrobe is another aspect of our lives that God wants us to submit to Him. I wholeheartedly encourage you to do so.

11

Career Choices

When I was a kid, as is often the case, I was sometimes asked, 'What are you going to be when you grow up?' The earliest reply that I can remember giving was, 'A policeman.' I'm not really sure why I said this, but I do remember it was in Year 2 of primary school and that there was a girl in the same class who said she'd like to be a policewoman. I worryingly thought, 'Does that mean I'll have to work with you?' Such is the reasoning of a six-year-old!

It is fairly pointless asking any kid of that age what they want to 'be' when they're an adult since they have such a limited knowledge of the jobs that exist (hence my unimaginative response). But to ask a kid today what they want to 'be' when they grow up is even more pointless. The idea that a child in today's world will grow up to have a vocation – one job or profession that they stick with for the majority of their working lives – is rather unlikely. It just doesn't happen anymore. Unlike for my parents' generation – and all those before them – these days someone finishing secondary school finds the world is a vastly different place than when they started education.

The pace of technological change, fuelled by the advent of the Internet and the limitless possibilities it brings, means the workplace is constantly changing like never before. Many of the jobs that the kids in my Year 2 class are now doing didn't exist when we were first asked that question. Even school kids with very fixed ideas about what they might like to do in the future can't really imagine how technology will change the way things are done and the type of job roles there will be by the time they start work.

As a result of this, my and all subsequent generations seem to be more confused than ever about what their 'career' might look like. If you're about to finish university, this dilemma may well be facing you. Even if you have a job already, the chances are that a few years down the line your job will change, or you'll want to find a different one, or you'll suddenly face unemployment. More than ever, the world of work has become an unpredictable environment. If you're starting out in work today, you might well have twenty jobs in your working life. You'll likely to need to retrain at some point. You'll probably still be working until you're almost seventy. And in those fifty years who can imagine how technology will change the world of work?!

So how can following Jesus help us think about making good decisions about our career? Considering all that I've already said in part two of this book, the most important question is not, 'What are you going to be?' Nor is it a Christian version of the same dilemma: 'What career does God want me to have?' As the world changes so much, you can't really plan ahead for the next ten or even five years. So let's make things simpler and think about just the first step: 'What does God want me to do now?' Does that seem a little less daunting?

To be honest, I'm not long into my working life myself. After university I took the slightly unusual step of working for my church for five years. Now I've retrained and become a maths teacher, something I never imagined doing almost until I applied! My first job was as a paperboy at thirteen. Since then I've had thirteen different jobs, which incidentally is the same amount as my dad has had in his entire career. When I was at school, I wasn't sure if I wanted to go to university, so didn't even apply and took a gap year first. When I finally went to university and studied economics and development studies, I still had no idea what I would do afterwards. But each step of the way God has guided me and helped me to make decisions. Here are a few things that have shaped my choices:

1. Prioritise being part of a Christian community

The Bible emphasises this importance a lot (Heb. 10:25). If we're faced with a career decision that affects where we live, we should think very carefully about it. Any job that would isolate us from a good local church would probably be very unwise to take. It might be a great job, but remember what our lives are really about. Our spiritual health should always come first. Nor must we for a moment think that we can 'go it alone' without a good church; that's not the essence of Christianity.

By a 'good church' I don't mean one that looks good or is cool or even is where people are warm and welcoming if they don't also truly prize the Gospel and love God. I mean a church that teaches the Bible faithfully, and where we can grow, serve and be honest with other Christians as we follow Jesus together. The church is Jesus' priority, He gave His life for her (Eph.5:25), so it should be ours too when considering career moves.

2. Consider where you would best serve Jesus

The Bible instructs us to work for God in a heartfelt way: 'Whatever you do, work at it with all your heart, as working for the Lord, not for human masters, since you know that you will receive an inheritance from the Lord as a reward. It is the Lord Christ you are serving' (Col. 3:23–24).

Given that it's difficult (though not impossible, as I will describe later) to do this for a long period of time if we're doing a job that we hate, it's generally wise to choose a career that we will enjoy. That may sound obvious, but there are a lot of people who end up doing a job they don't like. If we choose a career simply because it will earn us the most money, or because it give us the most power, or because it's convenient, or even because it's what our parents want us to do, we may end up not enjoying the job. It's not easy to get up each day and work for Jesus when what we have to do drives us up the wall. So find a job about which you can think, 'I could gladly do that for Jesus for years to come.'

It would, of course, be naive and unhelpful for me to suggest that everyone is able to do their 'dream job', especially if you're just starting your career. That's not what I'm saying. But the workplace is where we'll spend more time than almost anywhere else, so it makes sense to try to be in an environment we like. We shouldn't be afraid to go for something that we really enjoy.

3. Step out in faith
If you're not sure what type of job you would like,

push some doors and see what happens! Since God's will is not a certain career pathway, we don't just sit around for months agonising over the decision while waiting for God to write instructions in the sky. As I've said, God's silence may mean He wants you to take a step of faith first and trust that He will lead you once you're through the door. Sometimes the path of working out God's guiding comes through opening door after door – and it's only years later that you see the way God was using that process.

The story of Joseph reminds us that even unpredictable twists and difficult situations are not a problem for God. He loves writing epic stories from challenging or even mundane circumstances. Likewise our mistakes can be used by Him to shape us. God is the master crafter of our lives and is always working for our good. Therefore instead of worrying about the direction of our lives, we can trust it to God while we prioritise loving Him and becoming more like Him.

12

Work Attitudes

Whether we're employed in a job we've always dreamed about or one that is an utter nightmare, the reality for most of us is that there's nowhere we'll spend more time than the workplace. Although the decisions we make about which job or career to pursue are important ones, we're only faced with them at particular seasons in our lives. However, the way we behave when we're in our job is one we have to make every day and is as important to God. The Bible can and should inform our 'nine-to-five' just as much as any other part of our lives.

We are made to work

When God made people, He gave them a job to do. If you read the first few chapters of Genesis, you'll see that God gave Adam and Eve a role as gardeners, zookeepers and local rangers in looking after God's creation (Gen. 1:28; 2:15). It's helpful to pause and think about this for a moment. When we contemplate the paradise of the Garden of Eden, we might picture Adam and Eve with their feet up, sunbathing, drinking cool drinks and chatting with God. There may well have been some of that. But if you've ever met a gardener or a zookeeper, you'll know they work very hard and it's a demanding job to do. There's a lot of dirt, sweat and effort involved and little time for lazing around. God's original intention for humankind included work and there's nothing in the Bible to suggest that has changed.

In fact there are numerous warnings throughout the Bible about a lack of work leading to ruin. The book of Proverbs repeatedly refers to 'the sluggard' who is presented as a figure of ridicule and disdain (Prov. 13:4; 20:4; 26:15). Proverbs 6 states that the man who fails to get out of bed and to work will find poverty is just around the corner. You may think that is not so much wisdom as stating the obvious but it's amazing how many people, especially those between the ages of fifteen and twenty-five, consider staying in bed most of the day an appropriate use of time. The fact that you might have parents who take pity on you and avoid your financial ruin should not be an excuse to ignore the principle here. You're made to work, and laziness is disobedience to God's Word.

The New Testament drives the point home in a number of places too. In 2 Thessalonians 3:6 Paul writes, 'In the name of the Lord Jesus Christ, we command you, brothers and sisters, to keep away from every believer who is idle and disruptive and does not live according to the teaching you received from us.' We can infer from this that one of the issues in the Thessalonian church was idleness. Those who chose not to work immediately became reliant on other people for provision of every kind, causing a problem for the community. It might surprise you that the apostle Paul, who spent all his time sharing the Good News about Jesus and talking about spiritual things, would concern himself with – and in fact speak so strongly about – such an earthy and everyday issue as laziness, but 'being spiritual' doesn't mean shunning work – quite the opposite!

Paul goes even further when writing to Timothy with instructions to the church in Ephesus. He rids them of any mistaken idea that being a Christian means you can put your feet up when he tells them that failing to provide for your family is a denial of the Christian faith (1 Tim. 5:8)! It's worth pointing out that the meaning here is not just limited to the people living under your roof but extends to other relatives too. In a modern country with a welfare state in place and wider family who might live long distances from us, it can be easy to overlook this instruction, but it is a clear principle that applies to our work, whoever we are. We are not just to see our work as a personal fulfilment of any career goals, or even as earning money for ourselves and our futures, but as a means of having an income to provide and support those around us too.

Work is a God-given task for us to do for the benefit of society and especially our families. The reason Paul particularly gives this instruction here is so that the church can support people who are in real need but have no relatives to take care of them. He is underlining to them that it is each worker's responsibility to provide for himself and his family so that the church is not unnecessarily burdened.

This may seem a bit irrelevant to you at the moment, especially if you're at the beginning of your working life and do not have a family of your own, but it is a reminder that our work is not just about us. As soon as we start earning, we should adopt a healthy attitude to our income that reflects this outlook. Maybe God is channelling resources to you because there is someone else in your family who is unable to earn? If you do not have a family now, are you saving and planning for when you might in the future? What about making provision for looking after your parents in their old age? Again, that may or may not be an imminent prospect right now, but if even this idea causes you to scoff, it could be the case that you've been thinking about your work and earnings as a purely selfish enterprise.

The joy in awful jobs

Work is part of who God made us to be, so laziness and a refusal to take responsibility for others is disobedience. But how should we approach our job when we find ourselves in one that we don't enjoy at all? The good news is that God wants to bless us through everything we do (Rom. 8:28), so even if we have a job that really stinks, work in itself is still good for us.

Our immediate response to this idea, if we're in a job we really hate, might be, 'Not this one!' I can understand that. I've had bad jobs before. If this is not our experience now, it may have been before and is certainly likely to be the case at some point in our working lives. But being a Christian means a bad job can be especially good for us – even when it doesn't feel like it!

Of course there's no merit in pretending something is great when it's really not. Jobs that are endlessly repetitive, dull, stinky, tiring, uncomfortable or a terrible mix of all these things are no-one's idea of fun. Being a Christian in a bad job is not about smiling inanely and pretending everything is wonderful! But Jesus can change our attitude and make us think about our job in a different way.

1. Work is God-given and good

If we understand that work is God-given, we can appreciate it as a good thing. Even if we're working in a terrible job, we can take comfort from the fact that just by turning up each day we're obeying God and fulfilling an important aspect of what we've been created to do. Our particular task may seem meaningless and unimportant but we are not unimportant to God. The fact that He is smiling over us as we work can give tremendous meaning to what we do. When we're doing a job where we constantly think, 'What's the point?' we quickly begin to feel worthless ourselves. But as a Christian we derive our worth from our relationship with God and there is immense value in being aware of the pleasure of God as we work.

Seeing our work from God's perspective helps us to move on from just asking, 'What am I getting out of this?' Instead we can pray, 'Help me, God, to honour and obey You and know Your favour as I work today.' If we start praying that before each shift, we will start to feel differently about even the worse type of jobs.

2. We work for God's glory

As well as us being obedient to God's call on our lives by working, the manner in which we do our jobs can give glory to God too. Here is a principle that hopefully runs through everything I have to say in this book: what we do is not as important as how we do it. As Paul writes, 'Whatever you do, work at it with all your heart, as working for the Lord, not for human masters, since you know that you will receive an inheritance from the Lord as a reward. It is the Lord Christ you are serving' (Col. 3:23–24).

Here Paul is addressing the Colossian church that includes slaves as well as slave owners. He gives instructions to each group about how they should behave in the light of the Gospel. Since Paul doesn't take this opportunity to condemn slavery, some people mistakenly think that he – and by extension, God – is endorsing the practice. Yet this is a completely wrong conclusion to draw. Paul's point is that whatever we do, or whatever part of society we are currently in, does not matter as much as the manner in which we work. Even if we are in a culture that embraces slavery, this God-focused attitude should still prevail in the Christian. Although slavery in Paul's time was quite different to modern-day slavery, it was definitely not a position in which anyone wanted to be. But Paul knew that God didn't want them to see this as an excuse to adopt a poor attitude to their work. Even as slaves we are called to work for God!

Therefore, however mundane, demeaning and demanding our work might be, we do it first and foremost for God because this brings honour to Him. When people do terrible jobs with an amazing attitude and a servant heart, I actually think it brings most glory to God. Working in this way can most clearly demonstrate the characteristics that God prizes and praises in work: humility (Eph. 4:2), self-sacrifice (Matt. 19:29) and perseverance (Gal. 6:9). All of these are aspects of Jesus' life and we are reflecting Him when we show them ourselves.

I am sure that Jesus' 'job' of coming to earth and living amongst us was in many ways wholly unattractive. Despite this, He left the comfort and security of heaven to live in stinky, dirty houses and spend all his time with smelly people, many of whom were sick with every type of disease (Matt. 4:23). During His ministry He didn't even have a bed (Luke 9:58) as He went from town to town teaching people who tried to undermine Him (Matt. 22:18), healing people who were largely ungrateful (Luke 17:17) and being ridiculed, mocked (Luke 22:63–65) and ultimately killed by a group of people who were supposed to be worshippers of God (Luke 23:21). So we might turn our noses up at the prospect of cleaning toilets, but who are we?! The Bible says that at the end of the day we're just dust anyway (Ps. 103:14)! Jesus was and is the King of heaven and earth, the One who made everything and is perfect in every way (Col. 1:16).

Do you feel that your job is beneath you? Remember the One we follow, and be grateful that His humility and ultimate humiliation was for our sake. Jesus has given us a blueprint for a life of unappreciated, uncomfortable service. So we should be neither surprised nor outraged if at points in our lives we have to do a job that we think is a bit demeaning. Even if we end up doing an awful job all of our lives, the manner in which we work stores up eternal rewards for ourselves (2 Cor. 4:17). God is primarily concerned with the way we work rather than our job title or output. This is a key way in which the Gospel changes our view about what's important. We live in a world that prizes status and success but God prizes the process – our hearts (1 Sam. 16:7). The way we clean a toilet can put a smile on God's face.

The challenge of the workplace

We've seen that this principle of working for God first and foremost applies to whatever job we might have. Thus we can bring glory to God by cleaning toilets but also bring dishonour to Him as a CEO of a multinational corporation or vice-versa. The attitude of the heart described in Colossians 3:23–24 is not easy to keep up every single day we go to work. Moreover, Christians come under all sorts of pressure and temptations in the workplace to dishonour God with their conduct: gossiping; bending the truth; cutting corners; flirting; even treating our job as a 'god' and so spending endless hours working at the expense of everything and everyone else. For this reason it is important to have a strong conviction about why we are working and to remind ourselves often that the desires of our earthly boss come second to God's calling of what we are to be and do.

Most of the time, honouring God will mean honouring our boss too. God wants us to work hard and conscientiously to the best of our ability (Ecc. 9:10). Generally bosses or line managers value these things too! But sometimes our boss will ask us to do something that will be dishonouring to God. It's at those points our convictions are really scrutinised. Whose opinion do we really care about the most: God's or our boss's?

Being a Christian may well cause us to be incredibly successful in our workplace but it may significantly hold us back. Our faith may make us the cause of ridicule; it may even get us fired. We live in a world where in many respects the ways of the enemy have great influence. The Bible refers to the devil as 'the god of this age' (2 Cor. 4:4) so we shouldn't be surprised when being a Christian causes us to stand out and even creates problems for us. Jesus specifically warns us that we will be misunderstood and hated through our lives precisely because we're Christians (Matt. 10:22).

Having said that, it is also important to be wise and think carefully about what we say and do in the workplace as Christians. Being a Christian does not give us license to wag an accusing finger and take a stand on every ungodly practice that we might encounter. Our mandate is to live in the world but not be 'of the world' (John 17:14–18);

to acknowledge that the world around us is largely opposed to Jesus but not try to live completely apart from it. Neither has God given us a clear mandate to change the world through insisting on certain moral behaviour. Although this may seem commendable, it is not fruitful – people need to hear and respond to the Gospel before being convicted of the need to change their conduct.

With this in mind, let me end the chapter with a few practical suggestions for how to be a Christian in the workplace. First, as I've already said, we are to work hard and honour God in everything we do. The Gospel frees us from being a slave to the 'gods' of money, success and power but also warns us against idleness. It's sometimes a fine line between being diligent and being driven in an ungodly way but it's a road that Christ will help us to navigate if we let Him.

Second, we are to be open about our faith (2 Cor. 5:20). I find it helpful to tell my colleagues I'm a Christian early on in any job. Obviously this is not done as a big announcement – I'm not saying, 'Hey everyone, look at me!' But I find it helps to let people communicate this when I'm getting to know them as it can be more difficult to bring up later on. An easy way is to ask people what they did at the weekend and then, when they politely ask you the same thing, to say that you went to church. We are called to lead good lives so that others might see them and be attracted to God (1 Pet.

2:12). However, it will be impossible for the way we work to reflect the Gospel if we've not mentioned that we follow Jesus.

Third, and related to that, we should be intentional and prayerful about our witness at work. We are not told to take our workplaces by storm and demand that everyone repents. As we're on 'enemy territory' at work, that strategy is unlikely to be effective. But we are told to work for God and to always be ready with a reason for the hope that we have (1 Pet. 3:15). It's important to know what to say if people ask us about the way we live our lives. Do you know what you would say?

The workplace is such an amazing environment to meet new people and form great friendships, and it may well be our best opportunity to evangelise. Of course, we are there to work and so mustn't let our witnessing distract from this – if we're supposed to be talking specifically about an aspect of work, telling people about Jesus might well land us into trouble. But in any workplace there are appropriate times and places for chatting and getting to know our colleagues. We should pray about these regularly, asking God for opportunities to speak about Jesus and the right words to say when they come up.

Fourth, and finally, we must not compromise in following Jesus in the workplace. Just recently Christians have been in the news for witnessing and praying for colleagues at work, but the reality is that we'll always face opposition because we're people of God's kingdom and not the kingdom of this world (John 15:19). While we are to be wise in our work and witness, our call to be ambassadors for Christ is more important than any job we might have.

So we should not be afraid to be a Christian in the workplace and let our light shine. We are to be people of integrity even if everyone around us cuts corners. We must work hard even if everyone around us is lazy. We are called to speak the truth even if it's not what people want to hear. It is right to honour those in authority in our workplace (Rom. 13:5) but we are really working for and pleasing a bigger Boss and He comes before anyone else.

13

Healthy Living

We read in 1 Corinthians 6:19 that our bodies are temples, but this verse is often very misunderstood. Sometimes it is used to suggest that we should treat our bodies well – for example by not smoking, doing drugs or being overweight – simply because temples *should* be kept nice and clean. But I don't think that's quite what Paul has in mind when he writes this letter. For a start, we'll never get our bodies to a pristine, temple-like state of grandeur, however hard we try. More importantly, I don't think God wants us to make that our aim either.

Yes, our bodies are temples and so as Christians we should think about them. But the whole point of the temple in the Old Testament was that it was the place where God dwelt. If you went to the temple to look at how nice the brickwork was and ignored that

117

God was manifestly present, you'd have definitely missed the point. What Paul was trying to explain to the church at Corinth was that the way they lived their lives should have been a response to the reality that God had come to live inside of them. The Holy Spirit has come to make a home in and amongst God's people, just as God always promised He would (Ezek. 37:27).

So if what's going on inside us is most important, do our physical bodies really matter that much? The Corinthian Christians had decided that they don't. They claimed that they had 'the right to do anything' (1 Cor. 6:12) because they knew that they were forgiven and spiritually made new. They thought that how they behaved and what they did with their bodies was largely irrelevant to God. Even though they were believers in Jesus, they were committing numerous sins such as unfairly taking other church members to court, cheating each other and going to brothels.

It's important to notice that Paul's rebuking of them is not simply directed towards their behaviour. He does not say, 'Stop it! God wants you to be nice, clean, temple-like people.' Instead he reminds them that because Jesus has risen from the dead, God has come to live inside of them. Since God has moved in, they shouldn't think their bodies belong to them anymore (6:19). In fact God is now intimately connected to the physical things that they do (6:15). He doesn't tell them to stop misbehaving because they are being naughty; he wants them to grasp the bigger picture and comprehend that a much more profound change has occurred in them than they realise.

It's a mistake to think that God is concerned with clean-living as an end in itself. The Bible helps us to recognise that the entirety of who we are has undergone a radical change and we are to consider ourselves in a totally different light than before we met Jesus. Our bodies are important to God and therefore we should look after them, but rather than this being because that's the 'right thing to do', it's because God has made us, redeemed us and made His home inside of us by His Holy Spirit. The way we live and what we do with our physical bodies cannot be separated from God's intimate involvement with us. Seeing this big picture helps us to make good and faith-inspired decisions about our lifestyle instead of being motivated (or feeling guilty) from a sense of obligation.

Our health is one of the aspects of creation that God has entrusted to us to steward wisely. You may not have thought much about it before but God cares about our diet, exercise and the care we take of our bodies. Does that mean Christians should be 'health freaks' and shun anything that could be bad for us? Well, it's likely you'll become distracted from the primary goal of serving God and risk idolatry of some sort if you devote your life to having an 'ideal' body. The Bible never instructs us to become perfectionists and a pursuit like this is an unhelpful extreme. Nevertheless, although

God's Word actually says very little about the subject specifically, and this should cause us to be cautious about coming to definitive conclusions, it does consistently celebrate wisdom (Prov. 1:7; Col. 2:3; Jas. 3:17). We should therefore aim to use the measure of wisdom we have been given to make good decisions in this area.

We are fortunate to live in a society that knows more than ever about what is good for our bodies, hopefully leading to us enjoying a long and healthy life. That doesn't mean we should jump on every diet fad and fashionable fitness regime, but it does mean eating a sensible, balanced diet and exercising regularly. Even without the big picture of God being at home in us, living healthily is just common sense. Anyone with a sense of calling and purpose in life will want to look after themselves so they are able to pursue that goal for as long and as consistently as possible. If we're in the world to live for Christ and be His witnesses (Acts 1:8; Phil. 1:21), poor health is likely to hinder that in the short and long term. Now of course all of us get ill during our lives, sometimes for extended periods and most of the time we have absolutely no control over it. But there are some everyday decisions we can make about lifestyle, diet and exercise that can contribute towards or help guard against sickness and may have a significant effect on our life expectancy. Our everyday choices in these areas can impact the opportunity we have to be effective to God here on earth (Eph. 5:15–16).

As well as these potential long-term effects, there are also many temptations to sin that surround us when it comes to the type of lifestyle that we lead. The relative wealth, comfort and access to food and drink that most of us enjoy in this country is a great blessing from God that we should be grateful for. However, like all good gifts from God, they have the potential to be misused (Jas. 1:13–17). For example, the Bible highlights gluttony as sinful, not just because it is unhealthy but because it is a form of idolatry (Phil. 3:19). It may sound silly to suggest that there is a real danger of worshipping our fridges but, let's face it, the temptation is real. How many of us ever eat to make ourselves feel better? How real is the lure of a cold beer or a glass of wine after a hard day? And how easy is it for those things to be something we rely on? How easy is it to eat too much on a regular basis just because food is so good?! Cheesecake, chocolate, a can of coke or a glass of Pinot Grigio are all good things that we can enjoy but they can also all have addictive power. We should have our eyes open to this and reflect on our attitude to food and drink. If our desires for them are not kept in check, the Bible says they give birth to sin (Jas. 1:15)

It may sound as if I'm being a bit over the top here. Believe me, I don't want to spoil your enjoyment of food or drink at all – I certainly enjoy them! But I also know that they can be sources of temptation for me. I can look to them for selfish comfort and even escape when I'm feeling down rather than looking to God (1 Pet. 5:7). What's more, though I have insufficient expertise to talk in detail about eating disorders or the links between diet and struggles such as depression, I will say that we are physical, mental and spiritual beings and these aspects of us are intrinsically linked (1 Thes. 5:23).

Being physically healthy can help us to keep mentally healthy and it is vitally important that we talk about these topics together as Christians. In my experience we can be at ease when discussing deep spiritual matters in a small-group setting but everyone becomes uncomfortable when discussing physical life choices or mental health issues. Struggles with diet, ranging from occasional overeating to life-threatening conditions like anorexia, are not uncommon to Christians. We probably don't talk enough about these topics in our churches. This can contribute to the many Christians who suffer from them feeling ashamed about themselves and keeping hidden their unhealthy relationship with food.

For this reason I want to encourage us as Christians to try to be upfront and honest about our eating habits in the trusted context of the church so that, where possible, unwise steps don't develop into deeper problems (Gal. 6:1). I've found that Christians can be prone to frown upon unhealthy habits such as smoking but turn a blind eye to other aspects of unhealthy living such as overindulgence in food and drink. This is probably in part because we're British and the thought of challenging someone else's lifestyle, eating or drinking habits or especially their weight is extremely awkward and embarrassing. But as difficult as it may seem to address, we are called to be a real and genuine community (John 13:35). Sometimes a mistaken understanding of being polite can get in the way of being loving.

Discussions about healthy living should be part of any Christian maturity and discipleship. Of course, this can be a very sensitive subject and so it is important that any challenge or question that you bring to another believer is done in a suitable context of trust and honesty. Doing so with one or two trusted friends with whom you regularly meet up for mutual accountability is generally best (Jas. 5:16). Here are some questions that might be helpful to think and talk about:

- What steps are you currently taking to follow God's mandate to look after yourself?
- Are there habits or tendencies that you have in regard to diet, exercise or lifestyle that are unwise and unhealthy?
- Do you have anyone in your life who would helpfully challenge you if you were living irresponsibly?

I hope these will help you bring this very 'everyday' but very important area of your life under Christ's leadership (Jas. 4:7).

14

Marriage and Singleness

Walk into any church in this country and it will likely be full of married couples. If you're very new to Christianity, that might be surprising. In this day and age to see so many *married* couples, both young and old, is a distinguishing feature of churches. If you've been a Christian for any length of time and are not married yourself, you'll not only be unsurprised by this situation but may, at times, even be painfully aware of it.

We live in a society that's very confused when it comes to marriage. On the one hand, debates go on about the place of marriage in our society and who should or shouldn't be allowed to marry. On the other hand, the practice of marriage is becoming less and less commonplace, especially amongst the younger generation.

The fact that Christians seem to enthusiastically continue in this 'ancient practice' of marriage puts them more and more at odds with the culture around them. It also means that a higher and higher percentage of people in society who choose to marry are Christians. Therefore being married can be seen as a thing to do if you're 'religious' because those who aren't 'spiritual', by and large, are choosing not to wed. As a result, if you are a Christian and *not* married, you can feel less significant and even out of place in church.

The reality is that God has created marriage as a central part of His creation (Gen. 2:23–24). It's a significant part of the Gospel too for it is a beautiful and unique picture of Jesus' relationship with the church (Eph. 5:22–32). As I have already said, today marriage is still 'the norm' in the Christian church, as it always has been, and it is vitally important for the future of the church too. Marriage is a good thing. Yet not everyone will marry and not everyone should marry (1 Cor. 7:8). Those who are single may be a minority, but they are a significant one and sometimes, sadly, an overlooked one. Intentionally or unintentionally, churches cater for their largest demographic: married couples and families. This can leave others feeling left out or, even worse, that church isn't really for them. This is a real issue in our churches that we must work hard to address, and we all have a role to play.

If you've come through university, it's likely you'll have seen many of your friends pair off and get married. If you aren't married, as much as you're happy for your friends' own marriages, being single and a Christian can be really hard. While I'm not wanting to patronise anyone in this situation, I do want to acknowledge that being single in church can be a difficult, and sometimes lonely, road to walk – maybe not always, and maybe not for you, but it can be so nevertheless.

There is something in human beings that feels incomplete without the security of a loving relationship. God Himself said it was not good for Adam to be alone (Gen. 2:18); he needed companionship. But our desires actually stretch beyond the here and now because God has put eternal concerns in our hearts (Ecc. 3:11). Therefore our desire to be known, loved and befriended in a consistent, ongoing way will only be truly satisfied by God (John 4:14; 10:10; Ps. 16:11).

Having said that, marriage is a reflection of the love God has for us (Eph. 5:32). So if we are married, we experience the covenantal love, acceptance, companionship and security that comes from our commitment with our marriage partner as well as knowing God's love. If we're not married, we don't have this extra experience, which is hard. It may seem unfair that some people experience a present, tangible reflection of God's love (as imperfect as it may be, since none of our marriages reflect Christ's love for the church), and other people don't.

Wanting to be married is a good desire, because marriage is a good thing, but that desire can lead some people to disappointment and heartache for years and years. It must be a hard journey to walk, and although I am married, I imagine it can be a road with many temptations and potential feelings of discouragement and loneliness.

Only you can walk your path

As a married man I can sympathise but not empathise with those who are single in the church. But being single is a path that many Christians through history have walked too, not least several of the Bible's main characters, including the apostle Paul (1 Cor. 7:7) and Jesus Himself. Do you feel lonely in your singleness? In some ways Jesus was the loneliest person that ever lived. Do you feel rejected, overlooked, unlovely and at odds with those around you in your church? Jesus experienced all these things and is able to empathise with you.

Whether we're single or married, we all experience the temptation of jealousy. There's always part of us that looks at other people's lives and wishes we were in their shoes. There are those who are married who sometimes wish they were single.

One of the biggest challenges in life is coming to terms with the path God has set out for us to walk

(Eph. 2:10) when it doesn't look like a route we want to take. Our selfishness inclines us to believe there are certain things that God owes us in life. When other Christians around us are married, we're tempted to think that God's holding back from us if we don't find a spouse. When we become unwell, poor or without a job, or even get overlooked for a position in church that we feel we could do, there's a similar temptation to ask, 'Why can't I be like others and get what they have? What are You doing, God?' But in Christ God promises us eternal life (John 11:25) and to provide for what we need (Matt. 6:31–33). He doesn't promise us everything we want, nor does He say we will receive everything that other people around us have.

Just as in Jesus' parable of the workers in the vineyard (Matt. 20:1–16), we foolishly judge what is 'fair' by comparing ourselves to others. We forget that everything we receive from God is a gift and infinitely more than we deserve from Him. Sometimes we're quick to say, 'That's not fair', forgetting that Christ going to the cross was radically unfair and yet we are infinitely blessed by it as His expense. Faced with the Gospel, our response should be, 'Wherever you lead, Lord, I will gladly follow' – whatever cost it entails. So the question for us is, are we going to trust God to lead our lives? Do we recognise that only we can walk the path God has for us? Though it may look different from the path others are on, He has specifically marked ours out for our blessing (Rom. 8:28).

The world we live in likes to give us an illusion of control. It tempts us to believe that we can shape our lives in a detailed way according to our plans and desires. This is especially true when it comes to relationships – the world wants us to believe that if we only tried harder, looked sexier or achieved a bit more, then the woman or man of our dreams is only round the corner. Every romance in every film mixes together a strange concoction of heroic personalities and mysterious 'fate' that brings people together in an ingenious way. This tricks us into believing that meeting our 'soulmate' is inevitable. But it's a lie. A scriptwriter can control the destiny of his characters; it's not the characters themselves that choose their path. An advertiser, magazine columnist or blogger can tell us the 'tips to success' but all they really have to offer is words; they don't control anything nor have any power to shape our destiny. God is in control. He is in control of our lives. He has not empowered us to shape our destiny the way we would like it but has invited us to trust Him.

Despite what the media may try to convince us of, there's no guarantee of a 'successful life' other than entrusting it to God. We may get to live most of our lives with a spouse; we may not. Either way, we certainly won't meet our 'soulmate' now; once we've lived out our days in this life, our soul will go to heaven, where we won't be married anymore. Then when Jesus returns and brings together heaven and earth, we'll be united with our resurrection body and live in it forever. We won't be married then either (Matt. 22:30) – even if our spouse will also be there. The Bible gives us no reason to believe that our souls will be eternally intertwined with anyone else's. The only eternal bond we make is our unity with Christ Himself.

A greater gift: singleness or marriage?

Throughout church history the perceived value of singleness has fluctuated a great deal. Sometimes this has been helpful but at other times it has been tragically unhelpful, especially when so-called Christian teachers have forbidden marriage, something that the Bible specifically tells us not to do (1 Tim. 4:3). Such prohibitions have contributed to the most hideous of sins.

But the Bible does paint singleness in a very positive light. If we apply it correctly, valuing singleness can be a huge blessing in our churches. So far I have probably come across in a sympathetic manner but showing pity for those who are single – this is the last thing that I want to do. In Paul's letter to the Corinthians he contrasts the advantages of singleness against the 'divided' concern that being married brings (1 Cor. 7:32–35). Singleness is a unique way that we can live for God. We should not forget or underemphasise this.

In our lives it's important that we consider how any

decision might affect our devotion and obedience to Christ. Some conclude that to walk faithfully with God means to stay single even if the opportunity for relationships and marriage occurs. Others feel that they can or should fulfil what God has called them to in life by being married. Reading 1 Corinthians 7, it may be tempting to suggest that being single is *more* godly as we can pursue following Jesus and not have this so-called 'divided' concern. Certainly at times over the years this attitude has been popular. But is this a correct conclusion to make? To answer that we need to think about the context that Paul was addressing in order to fully understand how to apply this passage of the Bible.

Given the chaotic and difficult time that the church was experiencing in Paul's day, being a Christian put you in immediate danger. Reaction to this new 'religion' was unpredictable and even violent, and early Christians lived with a real sense that the window for evangelism was small. They knew neither whether Jesus would come back very soon nor whether the violent opposition to the church might become overwhelming. These were uncertain times to be a Christian.

It was because of this that some people reacted by saying, 'Forget about everything else, let's just be spiritual.' This led to some teachers prohibiting marriage and speaking against it. Paul therefore had to give corrective teaching in his letters by underlining that marriage was good and a blessing from God. Whether we are married or single, we shouldn't see one or the other as 'more spiritual'. Being 'spiritual' is the attitude of our heart towards Christ and this can be equally right or wrong whether we are married or not.

At the same time, in the context of the early church it was important to be realistic about the dangers new Christians faced. Was it a good idea to marry? Yes, marriage is a good thing! But there is a freedom and a particular devotion to world evangelisation that can be achieved by being single, as Paul himself exemplified. In addition, it was the case for almost all of the apostles that following Christ meant ultimately dying for the cause. Would it be a good idea for them to make someone a widow in just a few short years? A tough decision!

The bottom line is that it's important to carefully consider to what God has called us, whether it's singleness or marriage. Our most important task is to follow Christ (Luke 9:62). To hold up 'marriage' or 'singleness' as a better or more biblical alternative to the other in this is neither wise nor biblical. As I have said already, every Christian must follow the path that God has laid out for them.

Of course, this is not always easy to determine. Judging God's calling is a continuously challenging aspect of a Christian's life. Like any decision it should be thought through carefully and be fuelled by a mix of prayer, the words of the Bible, and advice from church leaders and Christian friends.

But, ultimately, whether God wants us to walk our path as a single person for some, most or all of our life, or whether God plans for us to be married, He will give us grace for this (Phil. 4:11–13).

God will not call us to do something that we can't manage. While we may not be able to manage it on our own, with God's help we will finish the race (Heb. 12:1–2). He also promises that we will not be tempted beyond what we can bear (1 Cor. 10:13). Whatever situation we are in, there will always be some level of dissatisfaction. Marriage is no picnic. Singleness can be dreadfully lonely. Divorce and bereavement can be scarring for life. But the good news is that all these ups and downs are just temporary. The surest antidote to the troubles of this life is to focus our attention on the promises of Jesus that go beyond our earthly existence.

I know that's much easier said than done, but it is no less true because of that. If we're honest, much of the disappointment and dissatisfaction that we sometimes feel is at least in part a product of us placing our hope in this life. We have many reasons to be happy in this life, but we have even more sources of joy when we consider what God has prepared for us for eternity (1 Cor. 2:9). Our life is not defined by whether or who we marry; it's defined by who we'll be united with for eternity. Trust me (or really, trust Him): it'll be worth the wait.

Conclusion

Trust in the LORD with all your heart
and lean not on your own
understanding;
in all your ways submit to him,
and he will make your paths straight.
Proverbs 3:5–6

When I was a child, we used to sing these verses in Sunday school, and their impact has stayed with me ever since. Sadly, they are not verses I have heeded at every stage of my life. I have fallen well short of them but God, in His mercy, has brought me back to His path. At other times I have clung to them and submitted my ways to Him, and that has made life tremendously difficult. But I can think of no better sentiment to pass onto anyone else about how to live in this world. This truth has proved true in my life and I am yet to meet a man or woman who has aimed to live by it and been disappointed. I know I never will.

In this book I have tried to explain and unpack what submitting your ways to God might look like in different areas of life. I pray this has been helpful to you, although I know it will never be comprehensive enough. Therefore, as I finish, I want to reflect on these verses and leave you with some guiding principles for all of life, whatever unique challenges and opportunities you will face.

1. *Trust* in God with all your *heart*

This is not a theme I have majored on in this book but I hope it is one that underpins all I have said. God wants us to obey Him, but out of love (John 14:23), not out of a sense of obligation or fear of punishment. Through the Gospel we see that God's intention has always been relational harmony with His creation: from the Garden of Eden, where God walked (Gen. 3:8); to God's call of Abraham who was known as 'God's friend' (Jas. 2:23); through the life of Jesus, who called His disciples 'friends' (John 15:15); and into eternity, where Jesus has gone to prepare a place for us in His Father's house (John 14:2).

Trust is a decision of the will, informed by the mind but made real by action. It is another way of describing faith. Intellectually agreeing with the biblical truth about God is important but it is not sufficient for the Christian life. We can say that we believe Jesus has died on the cross for us, forgiven our sins and saved us to be with Him forever, but if our lives look no different than those who do not believe these things, we are not truly trusting God at all (Jas. 2:17). God wants us to follow Him because we *know* Him, we have a deep and deepening relationship with Him, and because we trust He is faithful to His Word. In one sense, we should not make *obeying* God our aim in life. Instead, we should aim to trust Him, get to know Him and grow closer to Him, because by doing this our love for God will grow and obedience will be purely an expression of worship.

2. *Lean* not on your own *understanding*

This is a very difficult habit to break. To choose to follow God, even when our own reasoning, logic and feelings point us in a different direction, is an incredibly hard thing to do. It is the most radical aspect of what we are called to by God. 'Our understanding' is the way we see the world, the experiences that we have had and the knowledge that we have accumulated. It is very natural to make decisions based purely on this. But when we become Christians, we are opened up to a whole new realm of wisdom and God's truth will sometimes point us to a very different conclusion than if we were left to our own devices.

For example, it made little sense, humanly speaking, for Noah to build an ark (Gen. 6). Based on human experience, reasoning and logic alone, no-one would have thought it was a sensible thing to do. When Noah did so, everyone must have thought he had 'lost his mind'. We use this phrase to mean that someone's mental faculties have been dramatically diminished. It's the belief that someone has less intelligence, logic and reasoning than everyone else. But in the case of Noah, what looked like stupidity was actually caused by knowing *more* information than anyone else, not less. Noah was proved right in his decisions, with his wisdom a result of the fact he 'walked with God' (Gen. 6:9, ESV). Had others known about the impending flood, there would have been boats and arks built on every street corner, but everyone else lived in ignorance until it was too late.

As Christians, God has revealed to us *more* about Himself, life and ourselves than anyone else knows (Col. 1:27), and this means we can't carry on living like everyone else. We know too much to live just by our own understanding. Given that we know what life's really about, in all sorts of ways God calls us to build arks of our own – to take steps of faith that may look foolish to others but are in line with true wisdom.

3. Submit to *God* and He will make your paths *straight*

The call to submit to God comes with an amazing promise. A mistaken view of God is that He says to us, 'Submit to me ... or else!' Tragically this is a sinful lie that many people choose to believe and use as a reason to reject God's intervention in their lives. At points of decision and temptation it is an idea that comes to our minds too. But God never threatens us or tries to manipulate us for His own end. Yes, He tells us clearly about the consequences of our sin and rebellion against Him, but we know that Christ came into the world not to condemn but to save (John 3:17).

God invites us to submit our lives to Him and assures us that the journey of our lives will be a straight path. What does that mean? We see from the whole Bible that it does not mean our lives will be free from difficulty. Nor does it mean that we will be rich in financial wealth. No, God promises us a straight path, not an easy or materially prosperous one. A straight path is a path of purpose. A straight path has a clear direction and a clear destination. A straight path is a road that we walk alongside God and it is the path of life. Wouldn't you like your life to be described in the same way as Noah's? Genesis 6:9 is a short sentence in the Bible – 'Noah walked with God' (ESV) – but it says so much.

As I bring this book to a close, my prayer is that you make it your aim to walk with God all the days of your life. We all fall short in our obedience to God. Left to ourselves, none of us is able to keep on the straight path of walking with Him. But we can be encouraged that God has promised to *make* our paths straight. Even when we fail Him, we can submit ourselves again and know that our loving heavenly Father takes us by the hand and promises to never let go. There is no better promise to hold onto than that.

a division of 10 of those.com

10Publishing is the publishing house of **10ofThose**.
It is committed to producing quality Christian
resources that are biblical and accessible.

www.10ofthose.com is our online retail arm selling
thousands of quality books at discounted prices.
We also service many church bookstalls
and can help your church to set up a bookstall.
Single and bulk purchases welcome.

For information contact: **sales@10ofthose.com**
or check out our website: **www.10ofthose.com**